Cordon Bleu

Party
Cooking

Cordon Bleu

Party
Cooking

SPHERE BOOKS LIMITED
30/32 Grays Inn Road, London, WC1X 8JL

First published in Great Britain in 1972 by
B.P.C. Publishing Ltd.

© B.P.C. Publishing Ltd., 1972

First Sphere edition 1973

Designed by Melvyn Kyte
Printed by Waterlow (Dunstable) Ltd.

ISBN 0 7221 2507 0

These recipes have been adapted from the Cordon Bleu Cookery Course
published by Purnell in association with the London Cordon Bleu Cookery
School
Principal : Rosemary Hume ; Co-Principal : Muriel Downes

Contents

Introduction by Rosemary Hume

If good eating is a pleasure, cooking should never be a penance. We hope that this series of Cordon Bleu Cookery Books will give you ideas and help to take the chore out of cooking.

The recipes are selected from all over the world, and we have simply chosen the ones we like best. We hope you will like them too — not only the end result, but the cooking of them as well.

There are certain basic rules without which no cook can succeed, but beyond these the main ingredients to a successful meal are the enthusiasm and care that go into its preparation. Cordon Bleu cooking methods are basically French, and the French don't take short cuts. But this doesn't mean you have to be a slave to your kitchen; the correct methods, the right tools and enough practice will make you an efficient cook — which also means a speedy cook. Neither do you have to be extravagant; all the scraps that most English housewives would throw away — the chicken's feet, fish heads, odd vegetables — will be used in stocks to form the basis of tomorrow's meal. In fact, to emulate the French you must take pride in cooking with imagination, tempered with good common sense.

Cordon Bleu methods are a passport to rewarding and fascinating cookery. It is one of the few occupations that can be carried on in the home after marriage and motherhood. But no matter what your way of life, whether you are a housewife coping with everyday meals for several children, career woman running a home alongside office responsibilities, or single girl managing on snacks in a small flat — you will want to show off your cooking from time to time. Perhaps your husband may need to entertain business colleagues, or you might be called on to cater for a local women's committee lunch. It may be that your aunts, uncles, grandparents, nephews and nieces descend on you 'en masse' at Christmas every year. Whatever the occasion, if you can turn out a dish that is a little unusual, beautifully presented and tasting out of this world — your day, and theirs, will be made. But your success will depend entirely on the taste at the end — you can't get away with dressing up a badly cooked dish or a sad cake.

For this first book in the new series, we have chosen recipes for Party Cooking. These are the times that should be the most fun, but they also call for the most careful thought and planning beforehand. As one of the chief difficulties often seems to be judging the quantities required for a large number of people we have included guidance on basic catering quantities.

Once you have acquired a good menu for a large gathering it is very tempting to go on repeating it at every opportunity, so we have tried to choose some unusual ideas that will help you ring the changes. Some are traditional old English recipes that are rarely used now; if you can produce these you should create a sensation. Others are dishes from abroad of which your guests may never have heard, and they will surely appreciate this introduction to new tastes.

Whichever recipes you try, we wish you success. And try to enjoy your cooking, as that is halfway to being a good cook.

Notes and basic recipes

Almonds

To blanch almonds : pour boiling water over the shelled nuts, cover the pan and leave until cool. Then the skins can be easily removed (test one with finger and thumb). Drain, rinse in cold water ; press skins off with fingers. Rinse, dry thoroughly.

To shred almonds : first blanch, skin, split in two and cut each half lengthways in fine pieces. These can then be used as they are or browned quickly in the oven, with or without a sprinkling of caster sugar.

Aspic jelly

2½ fl oz sherry
2½ fl oz white wine
2 oz gelatine
1¾ pints cold stock
1 teaspoon wine vinegar
2 egg whites

Method

Add wines to gelatine and set aside. Pour cold stock into scalded pan, add vinegar. Whisk egg whites to a froth, add them to the pan, set over moderate heat and whisk backwards until the stock is hot. Then add gelatine, which by now will have absorbed the wine, and continue whisking steadily until boiling point is reached.

Stop whisking and allow liquid to rise to the top of the pan ; turn off heat or draw pan aside and leave to settle for about 5 minutes, then bring it again to the boil, draw pan aside once more and leave liquid to settle. At this point the liquid should look clear ; if not, repeat the boiling-up process.

Filter the jelly through a scalded cloth or jelly bag. Cool.

Bain-marie (au)

To cook at temperature just below boiling point in a bain marie (a saucepan standing in a larger pan of simmering water). May be carried out in oven or on top of stove.

Béchamel sauce

Using the quantities given in the particular recipe, put the onion and spices in the milk and heat gently, without boiling, in a covered saucepan for 5-7 minutes.

Pour off into a jug and wipe out the pan. Melt the butter in this, and stir in the flour off the heat. Strain in a good third of the milk, blend and add remaining milk. When thoroughly mixed, season lightly, return to the heat and stir continually until boiling. Boil for 2-3 minutes, then adjust the seasoning.

Court bouillon

2 pints water
1 large carrot (sliced)
1 onion (sliced)
bouquet garni
6 peppercorns
2 tablespoons vinegar, or juice of ½ lemon

Method

Put ingredients in a pan, salt lightly, cover, cool and simmer for 8-10 minutes.

Gelatine

As gelatine setting strength varies according to brand, it is essential to follow instructions given on the pack. For instance, Davis gelatine recommend 1 oz to 2 pints liquid.

Mayonnaise

To prepare $\frac{1}{2}$ pint mayonnaise, take 2 egg yolks and work in a small bowl with a pinch of salt, pepper and dry mustard until thick. Then add 2 tablespoons salad oil, drop by drop, until the mixture is very thick. Stir in 2 teaspoons white wine vinegar. Add the remaining oil a little more quickly, then a further $1\frac{1}{2}$ tablespoons vinegar. Season to taste with more salt and pepper as necessary.

Puff pastry

8 oz plain flour
pinch of salt
8 oz butter
1 teaspoon lemon juice
scant $\frac{1}{4}$ pint water (ice cold)

Method

Sift flour and salt into a bowl. Rub in a piece of butter the size of a walnut. Add lemon juice to water, make a well in centre of flour and pour in about two-thirds of the liquid. Mix with a palette knife. When the dough is beginning to form, add remaining water.

Turn out the dough on to a worktop dusted with flour. Knead dough for 2-3 minutes, then roll out to a square about $\frac{1}{2}$ - $\frac{3}{4}$ inch thick.

Beat butter, if necessary, to make it pliable and place in centre of dough. Fold this up over butter to enclose it completely (sides and ends over centre like a parcel). Wrap in a cloth or piece of greaseproof paper and put in the refrigerator for 10-15 minutes.

Flour work top, put on dough, the join facing upwards, and bring rolling pin down on to dough 3-4 times to flatten it slightly.

Now roll out to a rectangle about $\frac{1}{2}$ - $\frac{3}{4}$ inch thick. Fold into three, ends to middle, as accurately as possible, if necessary pulling the ends to keep them rectangular. Seal the edges with your hand or rolling pin and turn pastry half round to bring the edge towards you. Roll out again and fold in three (keep a note of the 'turns' given). Set pastry aside in refrigerator for 15 minutes.

Repeat this process, giving a total of 6 turns with three 15-minute rests after each two turns. Then leave in the refrigerator until wanted.

Watchpoint While you are making puff pastry, keep everything cool, and roll one way only to make sure pressure is even at all times.

Bake in a hot oven, at 425°F or Mark 7.

Stock syrup

Dissolve 1 lb lump, or granulated, sugar in $\frac{1}{2}$ pint water and boil steadily, without stirring, until sugar thermometer reads 220°F. Allow syrup to cool, then store by pouring it into a large, clean and dry screw-top jar.

Christmas and Boxing Day

On the following pages you will find a choice of recipes from which
to design not only your Christmas meal but much of your holiday
eating too. Don't forget to stock up well in advance (and in any case
not less than a week before Christmas) with all the canned and dried
goods you will need.

Quantities given for the Christmas Dinner are enough for six people
unless otherwise stated.

Christmas cake

8 oz plain flour
pinch of salt
$\frac{1}{2}$ teaspoon ground cinnamon
$\frac{1}{2}$ nutmeg (grated)
1 lb sultanas
12 oz seeded raisins
8 oz glacé cherries
4 oz almonds (blanched and shredded)
2 oz candied peel (shredded)
6 oz butter
grated rind of $\frac{1}{2}$ lemon, or orange
6 oz dark brown sugar (Barbados)
4 eggs (beaten)
2 tablespoons brandy, or rum, or sherry, or 1 tablespoon orange juice

8-inch diameter cake tin

Method

Line the cake tin with double thickness of greaseproof paper; set oven at 350°F or Mark 4.

Sift the flour with the salt and spices into bowl, then divide mixture into three portions. Mix one portion with the prepared fruit, almonds and peel.

Beat the butter until soft, add the lemon or orange rind and sugar and continue beating until the mixture is very soft. Add the eggs one at a time, beating well between each one, then use a metal spoon to fold in a second portion of flour. Mix in the fruit and then the remaining flour, spirit, sherry or fruit juice.

Turn the mixture into the prepared tin and smooth the top of the cake. Dip your fingers in warm water and moisten the surface very slightly.

Watchpoint This can be done with a pastry brush but great care must be taken as there should be only a film of water on the mixture. In baking, the small quantity of steam from the water prevents the crust of the cake getting hard during the long cooking.

Put the cake in the middle of the pre-set oven and bake for about $2\frac{1}{4}$ hours. After 1 hour reduce the heat of the oven to 325°F or Mark 3 and cover the top with a double thickness of greaseproof paper.

Test the cake after 2 hours' cooking by sticking a trussing needle or fine skewer in the centre. If it comes out quite clean the cake is done. Allow the cake to cool for about 30 minutes in the tin and then turn it on to a rack and leave until quite cold.

Wrap the cake in greaseproof paper or foil and store it in an airtight container for up to three weeks before decorating. It improves with keeping, but should not be iced more than a week before Christmas. Use glacé (soft) icing to ice cake and royal (hard) icing to decorate.

Almond paste

8 oz ground almonds
6 oz caster sugar
4 oz icing sugar (finely sifted)
1 egg
1 tablespoon lemon juice
1 tablespoon brandy, or sherry, or extra lemon juice
½ teaspoon vanilla essence
2 drops of almond essence
2 teaspoons orange flower water, or little extra cherry, or lemon juice
apricot glaze (see Maypole Birthday Cake, page 89)

Method

Place the almonds, caster sugar and icing sugar in a bowl and mix them together. Whisk the egg with the lemon juice and other flavourings and add this to the mixture of almonds and sugar, pounding lightly to release a little of the almond oil. Knead with your hands until the paste is smooth.

Brush or spread the cake thinly with hot apricot glaze. This coating makes sure that the almond paste will stick to the cake. Now place the almond paste on top of the cake; roll it over the top so that it falls down the sides (see photographs below).

Dust your hands with icing sugar and smooth the paste firmly and evenly on to the sides of the cake. Turn it upside down, press to flatten the paste on the top and roll the rolling pin round the sides. This gives a clean, sharp edge to the paste. Leave the cake in a tin for 2-3 days before icing.

Almond paste is laid on top of the previously-glazed cake, and rolled with a rolling pin so that it falls over the edges and down sides of the cake

Having smoothed the almond paste firmly and evenly on the sides, turn the cake upside down and roll round sides to give a clean, sharp edge

Royal icing

1 lb icing sugar
2 egg whites

This icing is not suitable for flat icing on sponge cakes because it would be too hard.

Method
Finely sift the icing sugar. Whisk the egg whites until frothy and add the icing sugar 1 tablespoon at a time, beating thoroughly between each addition. Continue this beating until the mixture will stand in peaks. Add flavouring and colour if wished. Keep the bowl covered with a damp cloth when piping.

Icing is made less difficult if a cake-stand with a revolving turntable is used

Glacé icing

4-5 tablespoons sugar syrup
8-12 oz icing sugar (finely sifted)
flavouring essence (and colouring as required)

Method
Make sugar syrup by dissolving sugar in $\frac{1}{4}$ pint of water in a small saucepan. Bring to the boil, and boil steadily for 10 minutes. Remove pan from the heat and when quite cold, add the icing sugar, 1 tablespoon at a time, and beat thoroughly with a wooden spatula. The icing should coat back of spoon and look very glossy. Warm the pan gently on a very low heat. (You should be able to touch the bottom of the pan with the palm of your hand.)

Allow sides of the cake to dry before roughly spreading icing over top of the cake with a plastic or metal 'straight edge' ruler (or palette knife)

Grapefruit and green grape salad

3 large grapefruit
6-8 oz green grapes
little sugar

For dressing
3-4 tablespoons olive, or salad oil
about 2 tablespoons lemon juice
caster sugar and salt (to taste
    pepper (ground from mill)
1 teaspoon fresh, or bottled, mint
    (chopped)

Choose thin-skinned and heavy grapefruit. Serve as a starter.

Method

Cut the grapefruit in half and prepare in usual way by cutting out the core with a serrated knife, then running the knife round the outside edge of the grapefruit, cutting between the flesh and the pith. Dip grapes in boiling water, then peel and pip. To remove pips easily, flick them out with pointed end of potato peeler. Put 1 dessertspoon of grapes in the centre of each grapefruit half. Dust with sugar and chill.

To make dressing : combine all the ingredients, whisk well. Taste and correct seasoning.

Pour tablespoon of dressing over grapefruit before serving.

Pears in tarragon cream dressing

3-4 pears
lettuce leaves (optional)
paprika pepper (optional)

For tarragon cream dressing
1 egg
2 rounded tablespoons caster sugar
3 tablespoons tarragon vinegar
salt and pepper
$\frac{1}{4}$ pint double cream

Use ripe, juicy pears such as Comice (one half per person). Serve as a starter.

Method

First prepare dressing : break egg into a bowl and beat with a fork. Add sugar and gradually add the vinegar. Stand bowl in a pan of boiling water. Stir the mixture until beginning to thicken, then draw off heat and continue to stir. When mixture has consistency of thick cream, take basin out of pan, stir for a few seconds longer ; season lightly and leave till cold.

Partially whip cream and fold into the dressing.

Peel pears, cut in half and, with a teaspoon, scoop out cores and fibrous threads which run from core to stalk. If using lettuce leaves, lay one or two on individual serving plates, breaking spines, so that they lie flat. Place half pear in centre of each, rounded side up. Coat each pear with 1 tablespoon of dressing. If using paprika, shake a little over the top.

The dressing can be made up (without cream) in large quantities and stored, when cold, in a screw-top jar in the refriger-ator. It will keep for 2-3 weeks. When needed, take out required amount and add cream.

Pork or veal forcemeat

1½ lb sausage meat, or half sausage
   meat and minced pork, or veal
1½ oz butter
1 large onion (finely chopped)
1 dessertspoon each dried mixed
   herbs and parsley (chopped),
   or fresh thyme, sage and
   parsley (chopped)
1 teacup fresh breadcrumbs
1 egg (lightly beaten)
stock from amount made for gravy
   (to moisten)
salt and pepper

Method

Put meat into a bowl. Melt
butter in a pan, add onion,
cover and cook until soft. Add
to meat with herbs, parsley and
crumbs. Mix thoroughly with
egg and moisten with as much
stock as needed. Add 2 good
pinches of salt and 1 of pepper.

Celery, apricot and walnut stuffing

1 small head of celery (thinly sliced)
2 oz dried apricots (soaked overnight)
4 oz walnuts (chopped)
1½ oz butter
2 onions (chopped)
1½ teacups of fresh breadcrumbs
1 tablespoon parsley (chopped)
salt and pepper

Method

Drain apricots and cut each half
into 3-4 pieces.
   Melt butter in a pan, add
onions, cover and cook until
soft. Then add celery, apricots
and walnuts. Cook about 4
minutes over brisk heat, stirring
continuously, then turn into a
bowl. When cool, add crumbs
and parsley. Season to taste.
These stuffings are suitable for
stuffing poultry.

Stuffing a turkey

1 *Stuff neck end*

2 *Sew up to keep in place*

3 *Use remaining stuffing in body
   cavity*

4 *Tie securely*

French roast turkey

1 turkey
pork, or veal, forcemeat (for the carcass)
celery, apricot and walnut stuffing (for the breast)
6-8 oz butter (enough to cover, depending on size of bird)
about 1 pint well-flavoured stock
1 rounded tablespoon flour (to thicken gravy)
salt and pepper

For garnish
8 oz rashers of streaky bacon
watercress
1lb chipolata sausages

Method
Set oven at 350°F or Mark 4. Prepare the forcemeat and stuffing (see recipes page 17), Undo trussing string from turkey legs, if necessary, and put the forcemeat into the carcass through the vent end. Re-tie trussing string. Loosen neck skin and push second stuffing well into breast cavity. Pull skin gently over stuffing and fasten under wing tips. A skewer can be pushed in to hold it firm. Put turkey in the roasting tin.

Spread butter thickly over a double sheet of greaseproof paper or sheet of foil. Lay the buttered sheet over bird and pour round half the stock. Cook for time given in chart (overleaf) according to weight.

Turn and baste bird about every 20 minutes, but keep paper or foil on while cooking. If stock reduces too much during cooking, add a little more. After 1 hour, cut trussing string holding legs.

Just before bird is cooked, prepare the garnish. Remove rind from bacon rashers, and wash and trim watercress. Grill bacon rashers and sausages.

To test if the bird is cooked pierce thigh with a skewer; if clear juice runs out, not pink, the bird is ready. Once cooked, set turkey on serving dish, pull out trussing strings and skewer, garnish with bacon rashers,

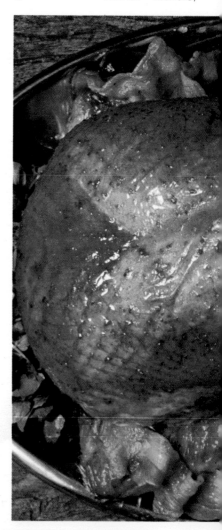

sausages and watercress, then keep warm.

If bird is not sufficiently brown towards the end of cooking time, remove paper and leave bird until golden-brown.

To make gravy: strain juices from roasting tin into a saucepan and deglaze tin with remaining stock. Add this stock to juices and skim off some of the fat. Put fat back into tin, stir in flour, then pour in liquid from saucepan. Stir until boiling. Season and strain back into saucepan. When ready to serve, reheat gravy and serve it separately.

See also Roast stuffed turkey page 74.

Roast capon

1 capon

pork, or veal, forcemeat (for the carcass) - see page 17

celery, apricot and walnut stuffing (for the breast) - see page 17

2-3 tablespoons good dripping

1 rounded tablespoon flour (to thicken gravy)

about ½ pint well-flavoured stock

salt and pepper

For garnish

6 oz bacon rashers (for rolls)

½ lb chipolata sausages

Method

Set oven at 375°F or Mark 5. Prepare the forcemeat and stuffing (see recipes, page 17). Undo trussing string from legs, if necessary, and put the forcemeat into the carcass through the vent end. Re-tie trussing string. Loosen neck skin and push second stuffing well into breast cavity. Pull skin gently over stuffing and fasten edge of skin under the wing tips. A skewer can be pushed in here to hold it firmly in place.

Melt dripping in a roasting tin, put the bird in, baste and cook in the oven for time given in roasting chart (see below), according to weight of bird.

Turn and baste bird about every 20 minutes. Just before the bird is cooked (test as for turkey, page 18), prepare garnish.

Remove rind from bacon rashers and roll up, holding each roll with a cocktail stick. Pierce sausages, grill with bacon rolls.

Remove capon from oven, set on a serving dish, pull out trussing strings and skewer, garnish with bacon rolls and sausages and keep warm.

To make gravy: pour off excess fat from roasting tin. Stir flour into tin, scraping well to mix in the sediment, then pour on stock. Blend, reboil and strain in a saucepan. When ready to serve reheat gravy and serve separately.

YOUR CHRISTMAS BIRD

BIRD	WEIGHT	SERVES	COOKING TIMES	
Frozen turkey	10 lb Oven ready	8-10	12 lb & under	15 minutes per lb 15 minutes over
Fresh turkey	13-14 lb Plucked	8-10	12 lb & over	10 minutes per lb 10 minutes over
Capon	5-7 lb Oven ready	6-8	5 lb & over	20 minutes per lb
Goose	8-10 lb	6-8	8 lb & over	15 minutes per lb

20   Note : weigh bird before stuffing

Duck with orange

4 lb duck
3 oranges
1½ oz butter
salt and pepper
¼ pint stock
1 wineglass red wine
1-2 tablespoons redcurrant jelly
watercress (to garnish)

For ½ pint demi-glace sauce
3 tablespoons oil
1 small onion (finely diced)
1 small carrot (finely diced)
½ stick of celery (finely diced)
1 rounded tablespoon flour
1 pint well-flavoured brown stock
1 teaspoon tomato purée
1 tablespoon mushroom peelings
   (chopped), or 1 mushroom
bouquet garni

Method

Place the thinly pared rind of 1 orange inside the duck with a good nut of butter and seasoning. Spread remaining butter over the breast. Truss the bird and place it in a roasting tin with the stock. Roast in a moderately hot oven at 400°F or Mark 6, for 15 minutes per lb and 15 minutes over, basting and turning the bird from time to time.

Meanwhile, prepare the oranges for the garnish. Cut them into segments, removing all the pith and membranes. Reserve any juice.

To prepare demi-glace sauce: heat a small pan, put in the oil, add the diced vegetables. Cook together on a low heat until the vegetables are barely coloured. Stir in the flour and cook slowly, stirring occasionally, until it is a russet-brown. Draw pan aside, cool mixture a little, and add ¾ pint of cold stock and the remaining ingredients. Season and bring sauce to the boil, half cover the pan and cook sauce gently for 35-40 minutes, skimming it when necessary.

Add half the remaining stock to the pan, bring it to the boil and skim; simmer for 5 minutes. Repeat this process with remaining stock, then strain sauce, return it to a clean pan and cook until syrupy.

Remove the duck from the roasting tin and keep hot on a serving dish. Tip off the fat from the roasting tin, leave the sediment behind, then add wine and orange juice; boil up well. Strain into demi-glace sauce, add redcurrant jelly and simmer until it is a syrupy consistency. Adjust seasoning.

Spoon a little sauce over the duck, garnish it with watercress at one end and with orange segments at the other. Serve the remaining sauce separately.

Spiced goose

1 medium-size fat goose (5-6 lb)
1 tablespoon salad oil
1 dessertspoon made mustard
1 tablespoon mushroom ketchup
1 tablespoon home-made fruit
   sauce, or tomato ketchup
1 clove of garlic (crushed)
oil (for browning)

For farce

2 lb minced pork, or beef
$\frac{1}{2}$ lb gammon rasher (minced)
liver of goose (minced)
1 tablespoon freshly chopped herbs,
   or 1 dessertspoon dried herbs
few drops of Tabasco sauce
1 teaspoon salt
1 teaspoon ground black pepper
1 teaspoon paprika pepper
1 teaspoon anchovy essence
2 oz fresh white breadcrumbs
2-3 tablespoons sherry

For braising

$\frac{1}{4}$ pint strong stock (made from the
   goose bones), or veal stock
1 large onion (sliced)
1 large carrot (sliced)
bouquet garni

For gravy

good $\frac{1}{2}$ pint strong stock (made from
   the goose bones)
salt and pepper
dash of tomato ketchup
dash of fruit sauce
kneaded butter (twice as much
   butter to flour, worked to a paste)
1 dill cucumber

For garnish

$\frac{1}{2}$ - 1 lb onions (glazed)
$\frac{1}{2}$ lb carrots (glazed)
about 2 lb small roast potatoes

To glaze vegetables : cook, covered in 1 teaspoon sugar, 1 oz butter and a pinch of salt, till tender, then cook with lid off till water has evaporated.

Method

Ask your butcher to bone out the goose, leaving the leg bones in, and lay it flat on a board. Mix salad oil, mustard and sauces together and add the crushed garlic. Spread this on the cut surface of the goose. Mix the ingredients for the farce together; season well and moisten with sherry. Spread farce over cut surface of goose, roll up and sew.

Set oven at 350°F or Mark 4. Brush the surface of the stuffed goose with oil then brown slowly in a large braising pan, or flameproof casserole, on top of stove. When brown, set goose on its back and pour round about $\frac{1}{4}$ pint of the stock. Add the onion, carrot and bouquet garni, bring to the boil, cover the pan, then braise in the pre-set oven for $2\frac{1}{4}$-$2\frac{1}{2}$ hours.

Meanwhile begin to prepare the garnish of glazed onions, glazed carrots and small roast potatoes. Prepare a separate gravy from the remaining stock, season well and add a good dash of tomato ketchup and fruit sauce. Thicken with kneaded butter. **Watchpoint** The gravy has to be made separately as it would be too fat if made from the cooking juices.

Shred the dill cucumber and add it to the gravy. Set aside. Lift out the goose, removing the trussing strings, and glaze under a grill to crisp the skin. Dish up the goose on an oven-proof serving dish, surround with the garnish of vegetables and reheat for a few minutes in a very low oven.

Duck with lemon compote

4-5 lb duckling
1-2 oz butter
salt
pepper (ground from mill)
2 sprays of rosemary
lemon compote
watercress (to garnish)

For stuffing

liver from the duck
2 chicken livers
1 shallot (chopped)
1 tablespoon chopped parsley
3 tablespoons chopped cooked
  mushrooms
2 tablespoons finely chopped
  cooked bacon
1 cup fresh breadcrumbs
1 egg (beaten)

Method

First prepare stuffing : dice livers and mix with rest of the dry ingredients. Season well and bind with egg. Fill into the bird.

Spread butter over breast and legs of bird. Truss and season lightly, cover bird with greaseproof paper; set in a roasting tin with the rosemary. Roast bird in a moderately hot oven at 400°F or Mark 6, allowing 15 minutes per lb and 15 minutes over, basting every 15 minutes.

When bird is cooked, remove and cool. When cold, carve and arrange on a dish. Garnish with watercress and serve with lemon compote (see right).

Lemon compote

4 lemons
2-3 sprays of tarragon
2 tablespoons sugar
3 tablespoons water

Method

Pare rind from 1 lemon, cut it into fine shreds, blanch for 5 minutes and drain. Slice peel and white pith from other lemons. Cut flesh across in thin rounds, removing all pips, and lay in a shallow dish. Dip tarragon sprays in boiling water; pick off leaves and scatter over lemons. Dissolve sugar in water, boil for 2-3 minutes to a thick syrup. Cool and pour over lemons. Serve chilled.

Potato and apple stuffing

1 lb potatoes
2 cooking apples
½ lb onions (finely chopped)
1 dessertspoon fresh or dried mixed herbs (chopped)
1 oz butter (melted)
salt and pepper

Method

Peel potatoes and put in a pan. Cover with cold, salted water and boil until cooked. Meanwhile put onions in a pan, cover with cold water and boil gently until tender (about 15 minutes).

Peel, core and chop the apples and put in a bowl with herbs. Drain the potatoes and onions and add to apple mixture with the butter. Mix well and season to taste.

Sage and onion stuffing

handful of fresh sage leaves, or 1 tablespoon dried sage
½ lb onions (finely chopped)
3-4 teaspoons boiling water
2 cups of fresh breadcrumbs
1 oz butter (melted)
1 large cooking apple (peeled, cored and diced)
grated rind and juice of ½ lemon
1 egg (lightly beaten)
4 pickled walnuts (quartered)
salt and pepper
stock from goose giblets (to moisten)

Method

Put onions in a pan, cover with cold water and cook until tender (about 15 minutes). Drain, turn into a bowl. Pour boiling water on sage. Leave to stand for 5 minutes, then drain. Chop fresh leaves, if used.

Add sage to onions, with crumbs, butter, apple, lemon rind and juice. Bind with egg, add walnuts and season well. Add a dessertspoon of stock if the mixture is too dry.

Cranberry sauce

1 lb cranberries
1 teacup of cold water
4 oz granulated sugar
about 1 tablespoon port (optional)

Method

Wash cranberries, put in saucepan, cover with cold water and bring to the boil. Simmer, bruising the cranberries with a wooden spoon, until reduced to a pulp.

Add sugar and port wine (if using). Cook very gently until all the sugar is dissolved.

Bread sauce

4-6 tablespoons fresh breadcrumbs
$\frac{1}{2}$ pint milk
1 small onion (stuck with 2-3 cloves)
bayleaf
salt and pepper
1 oz butter

Method
Bring the milk to the boil, add onion and bayleaf, cover pan and leave on the side of the stove for at least 15 minutes to infuse. Remove onion and bayleaf, add breadcrumbs and seasoning and return to the heat. Stir gently until boiling, then remove from heat. Beat in butter, a small piece at a time. Serve hot.

Brussels sprouts with chestnuts

1$\frac{1}{2}$ lb brussels sprouts
1 lb chestnuts
1 oz butter
$\frac{3}{4}$ pint stock, or bouillon cube with water
pepper (ground from mill)

Method
Skin the chestnuts by blanching quickly in boiling water and peeling off skin while hot.

Wash and trim sprouts and cook in boiling salted water until tender.

Put chestnuts in a pan with half of the butter and stock. Cover and cook until soft and the stock has been absorbed.

Meanwhile, put sprouts in a frying pan, add rest of butter in small pieces and shake pan gently until butter has melted, then add pepper.

Turn chestnuts into the pan and mix carefully with the sprouts. Put in a serving dish, and keep warm.

Christmas pudding

8 oz self-raising flour
1 teaspoon salt
½ nutmeg (grated)
1 teaspoon mixed spice
12 oz fresh white breadcrumbs
12 oz beef suet
1 lb demerara sugar
1 lb currants
1 lb sultanas
2 lb raisins (stoned)
4 oz candied peel
2 tablespoons almonds (blanched and shredded)
1 large cooking apple (peeled and grated)
rind and juice of 1 orange
6 eggs
¼ pint milk, ale, or stout

4 medium-size pudding basins, or 1 large and 2 small ones

Method

Well grease basins; have ready a fish kettle or sufficient large saucepans of boiling water.

Sift flour with salt and spices into a very large mixing bowl, add all dry ingredients and grated apple and mix well together. Beat eggs until frothy, add orange juice and milk, ale, or stout; add to mixture. Stir well. Turn into prepared basins, fill them to the top with mixture.

Butter a large round of greaseproof paper for each basin, cut a piece of foil to same size. Put both rounds together, foil uppermost, fold across centre to form a 1-inch pleat and lay over basins with buttered, greaseproof side next to pudding mixture. Tie down securely with string, leaving a loop for easy removal when cooked. Place basins in fish kettle, or saucepans, with enough fast boiling water to cover. Cook large puddings for 6 hours, small ones for 4 hours. Boil steadily, replenishing with boiling water from time to time.

When cooked, lift basins out carefully, leave foil and greaseproof paper on puddings until cold before retying with freshly-buttered greaseproof paper and foil and storing in dry cupboard.

Watchpoint It's important that puddings do not go off the boil.

Reboil the pudding on Christmas morning for 2-3 hours, according to size, replenishing with boiling water as necessary. Do not let pan boil dry.

When ready, take pudding from pan, remove foil and greaseproof paper and turn out on to a hot serving dish. If the pudding is to be kept warm for any length of time, replace basin over it to prevent it going dry. Keep warm.

Just before taking to the table, heat brandy in a small saucepan. Set alight and pour the brandy, flaming, round the Christmas pudding.

Serve with the brandy or rum butter.

Brandy butter

4 oz unsalted butter
4 oz caster sugar
2-3 tablespoons brandy (to taste)

Method

Cream butter thoroughly in a bowl, gradually beat in sugar and continue to beat until white and smooth. Then beat in brandy, a teaspoon at a time. Pile in a small dish or serving bowl and chill until firm. Serve with the Christmas pudding.

Rum butter

4 oz unsalted butter
4 oz soft brown sugar
2-3 tablespoons rum (to taste)

Method

Cream butter thoroughly in a bowl, gradually beat in the brown sugar and make as for brandy butter, substituting rum.

Mince pies

(makes about 18 pies)

For rich shortcrust pastry
8 oz plain flour
pinch of salt
5 oz butter
1 oz shortening, or lard
1 egg yolk
2-3 tablespoons cold water

For filling
about 1½ lb mincemeat
1-2 tablespoons brandy, or rum, or
  sherry
caster sugar (for dusting)

Pastry cutters, patty tins

Method

Sift the flour with a pinch of salt into a mixing bowl. Drop in the butter and cut it into the flour until the small pieces are well coated. Then rub them in with the fingertips until the mixture looks like fine breadcrumbs. Stir in the sugar, mix egg yolk with water, tip into the fat and flour and mix quickly with a palette knife to a firm dough.

Turn on to a floured board and knead lightly until smooth. If possible, chill in refrigerator (wrapped in greaseproof paper, a polythene bag or foil) for 30 minutes before using.

Set oven at 400°F or Mark 6. On a lightly floured surface, roll out half the pastry fairly thinly, and stamp into rounds (size to fit patty tins) with a cutter. Put rounds to one side.

Add trimmings to second half of the pastry and roll out a little thinner than first half. Stamp in rounds, a little larger than first.

Mix brandy, rum or sherry with mincemeat. Put larger pastry rounds into patty tins, with a good spoonful of mincemeat to fill well. Place smaller rounds on top, pinch pastry edges together, brush lightly with cold water, dust with sugar.

Cook for 15-20 minutes until nicely brown. Cool slightly before taking from tins.

Mincemeat

1 lb beef suet
1 lb cooking apples
8 oz mixed peel (shredded)
1 lb raisins stoned
1 lb sultanas
1 lb currants
2 tablespoons dried almonds
  (shredded)
12 oz demerara sugar
1 teaspoon mixed spice
grated rind and juice of 1 lemon
¼ pint rum, brandy or whisky

Method

Remove skin and shred suet; peel, core and chop apples coarsely. Shred peel. Mix suet, apple, peel and raisins together and pass through a mincer. Add remaining ingredients and mix well. (Alcohol gives mincemeat its keeping qualities.) Pack into clean, dry preserving jars with screw-top lids. Store in a dry larder.

Trifle

1 packet of sponge cakes (6-8)
3-4 tablespoons raspberry, or strawberry jam, or 1 packet frozen raspberries
5 tablespoons (2½ fl oz) sherry, or fruit juice
1 pint ready-made custard (sweetened with 3 tablespoons caster sugar)
¼-½ pint double cream

For decoration

blanched and split almonds (see page 9)
glacé cherries
diamonds of angelica

If children don't like the taste of sherry, use fruit juice.

Method

Split sponge cakes in two, sandwich together with jam and put in the bottom of a glass bowl. If using frozen raspberries instead, thaw as instructions on packet, put half split sponge cakes in the bowl, spoon raspberries over them, and arrange remaining cakes on top. Soak with sherry or fruit juice. Prepare sweetened custard and pour, while still hot, over trifle mixture. Then leave till cold.

Lightly whip cream and spread some of it in a layer over custard. Beat rest until stiff and pipe in a lattice work pattern over top. Decorate with almonds, cherries and angelica.

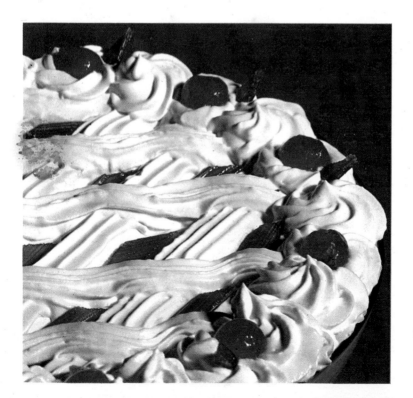

Braised goose (or capon)

1 young, tender ('green') goose, or
 capon — 5-6 lb

For farce

1 lb minced pork, or sausage meat
1 cup fresh white breadcrumbs
1 dessertspoon dried herbs
1 tablespoon fresh parsley
1 medium-size onion
1 oz butter
salt and pepper
pinch of ground mace
1 egg (beaten)

For braising

little dripping, or butter
2 onions (sliced)
2 carrots (sliced)
1 turnip (diced)
2-3 sticks of celery (sliced)
bouquet garni
6 peppercorns
$\frac{3}{4}$ - 1 pint good brown stock
1 wineglass red wine

For brown sauce

1 tablespoon each finely diced carrot
 and onion
1 stick of celery (diced)
1-2 tablespoons dripping
1 tablespoon flour
1 teaspoon tomato purée
$\frac{1}{2}$ - $\frac{3}{4}$ pint stock
2 wineglasses red wine
little slaked arrowroot
 (optional)

For garnish

braised chestnuts (see right)
$\frac{1}{2}$ - $\frac{3}{4}$ lb chipolata sausages (fried)

Method

Set oven at 350-375°F or
Mark 4-5.

To make the farce: mix the
meat, crumbs and herbs together in a basin. Chop the
onion and cook in a pan with
the butter until soft, then add
to the mixture. Season well, add
mace and bind with the egg.

Stuff the goose with farce
and truss. Rub a braising pan,
or flameproof casserole, with a
little dripping or butter. Put the
braising vegetables in this,
cover and sweat for 5-7
minutes. Then put the goose on
top and the bouquet garni and
peppercorns at the side. Add the
stock. Raise the heat and allow
the liquid to reduce by about a
quarter, then add the wine;
cover the bird with a piece of
paper and then the lid and cook
gently in the pre-set oven for
about 2 hours, basting fre-
quently. After about $1\frac{1}{2}$ hours,
remove the lid and continue to
cook, basting well and adding a
little more stock if necessary,
until the goose is nicely crisp.

Meanwhile prepare the brown
sauce by cooking the diced
vegetables in 1-2 tablespoons
of dripping. When barely
coloured, stir in the flour and
continue to cook to a russet-
brown. Then draw aside and
add the tomato purée and
stock. Bring to the boil and
simmer, with the pan half
covered, for about 30 minutes.
Then add the wine and continue to cook uncovered for a
further 20 minutes. Strain, rinse
out the pan and return the sauce
to it; set aside.

Take up the goose, place it
on a large meat dish and keep

Baked ham

warm. Strain off the liquid and skim thoroughly to remove the fat. Add the liquid to the brown sauce, then boil gently, to reduce, until it has a good flavour (5-6 minutes). Thicken if necessary with arrowroot slaked in a little cold water. Pour a little of this sauce round the goose and surround with the garnish of fried chipolata sausages and braised chestnuts. Serve remaining sauce in a sauce boat.

Braised chestnuts

Put 1 lb chestnuts in a pan, cover them with cold water and bring to the boil. Draw pan aside ; take out the nuts one at a time and strip off the outer and inner skin. When all the nuts are skinned, put them in a stew pan, cover with about $\frac{3}{4}$ pint jellied stock, season lightly, put the lid on the pan and simmer until the nuts are tender (about 20-30 minutes). Then take off the lid and increase the heat to reduce any remaining stock. The nuts should be nicely glazed.

Many people consider ham an essential part of the Christmas table. One method, which keeps the ham full of flavour and makes it more succulent, is to bake it in a flour and water crust.

For this you will need a 10-11 lb ham. Scrape it well, removing any rust from the underside, and soak it in plenty of cold water for about 12 hours, or overnight. Change the water if time permits. Then drain off the water, scraping the underside again, and dry.

Set oven at 325-350°F or Mark 3-4. Make a flour and water paste of a spreading consistency (about 2 lb flour to 1 pint water). Spread this thickly over and under the ham, put it in a large roasting tin and set in the pre-set moderate oven. Cook for about $4-4\frac{1}{2}$ hours. When done, carefully pull off the crust, removing the skin. If serving cold, cover with browned crumbs. For a party, serve hot with vegetables to choice ; braised onions, glazed carrots, and glazed parsnips go well with a hot ham.

Goose in aspic

1 small goose
2 onions (1 stuck with 1-2 cloves)
1-2 carrots (quartered)
large pinch of herbs
$\frac{1}{2}$ teaspoon allspice berries
(lightly bruised)
pared rind and juice of $\frac{1}{2}$ lemon
2-3 pints good jellied stock, or
1 calf's foot, or 2 pig's trotters
(split) and cold water
salt
1 oz gelatine
2 egg whites
3-4 drops of Tabasco sauce

For garnish
2-3 eggs (hard-boiled)
dill cucumber
watercress, or small cress, or
lettuce

*8-9 inch diameter cake tin, or deep
sandwich tin*

Start to prepare this dish the day before it is to be served. It can also be made with duck or chicken.

Method
Truss the goose, put into a large pan with the vegetables, add herbs, spices and lemon rind and pour in the stock (or water and calf's foot, or pig's trotters). The liquid should come almost level with the breast of the goose. Season with a little salt, cover and bring to the boil. Simmer for about 1-1$\frac{1}{2}$ hours, or until the goose is tender, skimming the liquid fairly frequently. When done, cool the goose a little in the liquid, then take it out.

Strain the stock and leave until quite cold. Remove any grease and measure stock (there should be about 2 pints, set to a light jelly). Pour this into a pan, warm it and then add the gelatine, the two egg whites, lightly frothed, lemon juice and Tabasco. Then continue to whisk the liquid backwards until it boils. Draw pan aside and allow contents to settle.

Watchpoint The jelly must be well seasoned and slightly sharp. Add more lemon juice and more Tabasco, if necessary, before clarifying.

Pour mixture into a basin through a cloth wrung out in boiling water. Take up the liquid and pour it through the cloth once more.

Skin the goose, cut the meat from the breast in one piece and slice the meat from the legs. Pour a little of the cool jelly into cake tin. When just about set, decorate with sliced hard-boiled eggs and sliced cucumber. If preferred, the whites and yolks may be separated and used to decorate in that way. Pour over another $\frac{1}{4}$-$\frac{1}{2}$ inch layer of cool jelly and allow just to set. Slice the rest of the goose and arrange in tin with breast and leg meat. Strain over enough of the jelly to cover it completely and put aside to set. To turn out, dip the tin into hot water, wipe it and turn jellied goose on to a serving dish. Garnish with watercress, small cress, or lettuce.

Baked stuffed ham

1 ham (weighing 9-10 lb)
root vegetables and pinch of herbs
(to flavour)
2 eggs yolks
6-7 tablespoons browned crumbs
dripping, or butter (for browning)

For stuffing

1 medium-size onion
2 oz butter
6-8 oz fresh white breadcrumbs
1 dessertspoon mixed dried herbs
salt and pepper

Method

After soaking, simmer the ham with water to cover well, add root vegetables and a pinch of herbs to flavour. Add a wisp of hay if available; this gives additional flavour. Allow 15 minutes per lb and 15 minutes over for cooking time. When the ham is cooked take it up, drain and peel off the skin. Cut the ham in slices down to the bone (leave the slices attached to the bone).

Set oven at 350-375°F, or Mark 4-5. To make stuffing, soften onion in a pan with the butter and mix with the crumbs and herbs; season well. Sandwich this stuffing between the slices of ham, reshape, then brush well with the egg yolks and sprinkle thoroughly with the browned crumbs. Put in a roasting pan with a little melted dripping, or butter, and bake in the pre-set moderately hot oven, basting occasionally, until the coating of crumbs is nicely brown and crisp (about 20-30 minutes). Serve hot with a vegetable.

Watchpoint If preferred, only half or part of the ham may be sliced and stuffed so that the rest of the ham could be left plain for eating cold.

Boar's head

1 large fresh, or salted, pig's head
oil (for roasting)

For farce
1 medium-size onion (finely
   chopped)
1 oz butter
2 lb pork (minced)
1 lb liver (minced)
brains from head
1 teaspoon black pepper (ground
   from mill)
½ teaspoon allspice (ground from
   mill)
1 glass sherry
tongue from head (simmered until
   tender)
1 tablespoon pistachio nuts
   (blanched and shredded, see
   page 9, adding pinch bicarbonate to water)

For decoration
½ - 1 pint meat glaze (made from
   bones and coloured with a little
   caramel, or gravy browning)
eyes from head, or white of 1 hard-
   boiled egg and 2 black olives, or
   prunes
2 curved sticks of celery, or cleaned
   bones from head (for 'tusks')
about 2 oz lard (creamed)
1 red camellia, or red paper flower
wreath of bay, or rosemary

This dish used to be famous as
a centre-piece for the Christmas
table, when the boar's head was
salted, boned out and filled
with a meaty farce. After the
head was cooked and reshaped,
it was lightly pressed and
decorated. A mixture of lard
and soot was then rubbed into
the skin to give the head its
traditional grey colour. The
drawback to this was that the
sooty skin had to be sliced
away before the head was
carved for serving.

Nowadays a pig's head is
used and is finished with meat
glaze.

Method

Ask your butcher to bone out
the head and rinse it. Remove
the eyes and reserve (if using
as decoration) but leave on the
ears. Use the bones to make
a strong jelly stock (this can
be done in a pressure cooker).
Colour the stock with a little
caramel, or gravy browning, and
use it for glaze.

Set oven at 350°F or Mark 4.
To prepare the farce: soften
chopped onion in butter in a
pan. Put the minced pork,
liver, brains and onion in a
bowl. Add pepper and allspice,
mix well and moisten with the
sherry. Skin the tongue (by
nicking the underside and peeling off carefully) and cut in
strips, or mince, and add to the
farce.

Spread the boned head, skin
side down, on a board, cover
with the farce and lay the
strips of tongue down the
centre. Sprinkle over the
shredded pistachios, then reshape the head and sew it up
with fine string. Brush with oil
and roast in the pre-set oven
for 3-4 hours, basting with the
fat that runs from the head.
When golden-brown, take out
and press the sides and end of
the head with boards and
weights. Leave until the next
day. Remove string and brush
with the glaze to give a good
shiny surface. It is essential to
try and keep the head in its
original shape.

Boil the eyes for about 5

minutes and, when cool, replace them in the head. Alternatively, make the eyes with white of a hard-boiled egg (if wished, this can be tinged with pink) and place the black olives, or prunes, in the centre to form the pupils. Stick the bones, or curved pieces of celery, in the head for tusks. Using a cone of greaseproof paper, decorate with the lard as shown in photograph. Place the camellia below one ear.

Serve on a large plate, or board, raised above the table (eg. on a wedding cake stand) and surround with a wreath of bay and / or rosemary. To slice, it is usual to start at the back of the head and cut down the sides of the cheek.

Sucking pig

In the olden days this used to be a great speciality for Christmas and other festive seasons of the year. It was then considered a fairly economical joint as piglets were often eaten when it was not practical to raise the full litter. The piglets were killed at 4-6 weeks old, then scalded and well scraped before being paunched. After this was done, they were wrapped in a wet cloth and kept in a cool place ready for use. Nowadays sucking pig is not such a cheap joint — being more of a luxury for Christmas. It is possible to order one from a butcher or provision merchant.

Roasting

If you have to dress it yourself, set the pig's forelegs forward straight out from the carcass, and the hind legs out backwards in the same manner.
Note: if your oven is not large enough to accommodate the pig's legs in this manner, they may be tucked under (see photograph on the right).

Set oven at 400°F or Mark 6. Clean and wipe pig thoroughly and fill it with the chosen stuffing (see page 38), packing it in well, and sew up. Set the pig in a roasting tin and brush over 1-2 tablespoons of oil or dripping (to make the crackling crisp). Roast in pre-set oven for $1\frac{1}{2}$- 2 hours, according to weight, basting frequently. Halfway through cooking, dredge with flour and continue basting.

Serving

Traditionally, the pig is served whole with a lemon in its mouth and the dish is surrounded with bay or fresh herbs.

However, to many people this is distasteful. If this is the case, the pig can be carved before serving. To do this, remove the head and split it, then split the body down the chine. Carve the shoulder and legs with a

circular movement of the knife round the joint and cut loin across into 2-3 pieces.

The meat can be served hot or cold. As it is very delicate and rich, it should be accompanied by a sharp sauce (eg. apple, or cranberry, or barbecue) and brown gravy, well spiced with mushroom ketchup. Baked apples are sometimes served with this dish (see page 39). If the pig is served cold, accompany it with a cold apple sauce. ▶

Sucking pig accompaniments

There are two main types of stuffing for sucking pig. The first is sage and onion and the other is made with kidneys and liver flavoured with marjoram.

Stuffing 1

2 Spanish onions
8 oz fresh white breadcrumbs
2-3 tablespoons freshly chopped sage
1½-2 oz butter
salt and pepper

Method
Trim and peel the onions, blanch them whole in a pan and then boil gently until just tender (this will take 20 minutes-1 hour, depending on size). Drain them well and press to extract any water; then cool and chop. Put into a bowl with crumbs and sage. Warm the butter until just melted, then add to the bowl. Season and mix well.

Stuffing 2

1 medium-size onion (finely chopped)
2 oz butter
liver and kidneys of the pig (minced, or finely diced)
8 oz fresh white breadcrumbs
2 tablespoons chopped marjoram
2 tablespoons chopped parsley
salt and pepper
1 egg (beaten)

Method
Soften the onion in the butter, then add the prepared liver and kidneys; sauté over brisk heat for 2-3 minutes, then turn into a bowl and cool. Add crumbs and herbs. Season well and stir in the beaten egg.

Stuffing the sucking pig before sewing it up ready for roasting

Baked apples with apricot

6 medium-size cooking apples
3 tablespoons soft brown sugar
grated rind and juice of 1 large
    lemon
1 oz butter
2 tablespoons dried apricot purée,
    or home-made apricot jam

Method

Set oven at 375°F or Mark 5. Wipe the apples and core them well. With the peeler, pare off about $\frac{1}{2}$ inch of the peel from the top of each apple. Mix sugar, lemon juice, rind and butter together and pack this into the cavities. Set apples in a baking dish and pour in just enough hot water to cover the bottom, then bake whole until tender (about 25-30 minutes, depending on size).

Cool slightly, then carefully scoop out about 1 tablespoon or more of the soft apple, taking care not to break or mis-shape the skins. Put this pulp into a bowl and adjust to taste, adding a little more sugar and lemon juice if necessary. Add the apricot purée. Fill the apples with this and reheat. Serve them hot with the sucking pig.

Filling apples with the butter and sugar mixture before baking

Orange and brazil nut salad

4 large oranges
2-3 oz brazil nuts (shelled)
1 lettuce (crisp), or 1 curly endive

For dressing
French dressing
1 shallot (finely chopped)
1 dessertspoon parsley
  (chopped)

Method
Peel the oranges, then slice them into thin rounds. Grate nuts with a cheese grater. Wash and dry lettuce or endive.

Place lettuce in a salad bowl with orange slices on top; scatter with nuts.

Spoon over French dressing, mixed with shallot and parsley. Chill before serving.

If preferred, the nuts may be left whole, soaked for an hour, then thinly sliced lengthwise.

French dressing

1 tablespoon vinegar (red or white wine, or tarragon)
½ teaspoon salt
½ teaspoon black pepper (ground from mill)
fresh herbs (chopped — thyme, marjoram, basil or parsley) — optional
3 tablespoons olive oil, or groundnut oil

Method
Mix vinegar with the seasonings, add oil and when the dressing thickens, taste for correct seasoning. More salt should be added if the dressing is sharp yet oily. Quantities should be in the ratio of 1 part vinegar to 3 parts oil.

Chicory, apple and walnut salad

1 lb chicory
2 dessert apples (preferably Cox's orange pippins)
2 oz walnuts (shelled)

For dressing

1 tablespoon wine vinegar
salt, pepper and sugar (to taste)
2 tablespoons salad oil
2 tablespoons single cream

Method
Wipe the chicory, remove any damaged leaves, cut across in thick slices and place in a salad bowl. Cut apples in four, remove core, slice and put into bowl without peeling. Add walnuts and mix well.

Prepare the dressing by mixing the vinegar with the seasonings in a bowl and whisking in the oil and cream.

Pour dressing over salad and mix well. Chill.

Salted almonds

½ lb Jordan almonds (skinned)
about 2 tablespoons salad oil
coarse kitchen salt

Method
Skin almonds by blanching quickly in boiling water, peeling off skins and drying well. Heat oil in frying pan, add half the almonds and fry gently until golden on all sides.

Lift from pan with a draining spoon on to absorbent paper which has been first sprinkled liberally with salt. Turn around in the salt immediately.

Add extra oil to pan if necessary and fry second batch of almonds in the same way.

Watchpoint Almonds must be coated in salt while they are still sizzling and hot.

Spiced fruit punch

1 bottle of port, or sherry
1 can orange juice (19 fl oz)
1 can pineapple juice (19 fl oz)
about 1 pint white wine
1 tablespoon sugar
2 strips of lemon peel
1-inch piece of stick cinnamon
2 oranges (sliced)

Method
Put all the ingredients except the sliced oranges into a large pan. Simmer for 3-4 minutes. Remove lemon peel and cinnamon stick, pour into punch bowl, add orange slices. Serve with a ladle into warm glasses.

Celery sticks

1 large head of celery
4 oz cream cheese
1-2 tablespoons top of milk
salt
pepper (ground from mill)
paprika pepper

Method
Wash celery thoroughly and cut sticks into 3-inch lengths. Soften cheese with top of the milk, add seasoning and mix well. Fill celery sticks with cheese mixture and dust with paprika pepper.

Cheese rolls

1 sliced loaf (thinly cut)
about 4 oz cheese (grated)
4 oz butter (melted)
paprika pepper

The flavour of the cheese is improved if a little Parmesan is included.

Method
Set oven at 400°F or Mark 6. Remove crusts from bread and flatten each slice by rolling very firmly with a rolling pin. Brush with a little of the butter, dust with cheese and paprika and roll up.

Put rolls in a baking tray and brush well with more butter. Bake about 10 minutes, then turn over, brush with remaining butter, and continue cooking until really crisp and golden-brown. Serve hot.

New Year's Eve

The most popular parties for New Year's Eve are the informal Buffet type — starting late enough to 'see the New Year in'. Plan food that is easy to eat with a fork. Have one big dish with salads to accompany and rice or hot baked or chip potatoes. Drinks could include mulled wine or hot or cold punches and hot soup should be on the menu if the weather is cold. The following recipes are for 12 people unless otherwise stated.

Bortschok

2 lb shin of beef
4 pints water
2 onions (1 stuck with a clove)
large bouquet garni
parsley stalks
1 bayleaf
stick of celery
strip of lemon peel
6 peppercorns
1 teaspoon salt
3 large cooked beetroots
1 can consommé (optional)
9½-10 fl oz soured cream
    (optional)

Method

Cut up the beef into small pieces and put in a large pan with three-quarters of the water; bring slowly to the boil, and add the remaining water in two parts. This addition of cold water brings the scum more rapidly to the surface and makes the broth clear. When on boiling point and well skimmed, put in the rest of the ingredients (except the beetroot, consommé and soured cream), partly cover the pan and allow to simmer for about 3 hours.

Note: if using a solid fuel cooker, cover the pan completely and put in the cool oven overnight.

Strain the broth and return to a clean pan. Grate the beetroot and add to the broth. Cover the pan and leave to infuse on low heat for about 40 minutes. Test for seasoning: the soup should not taste sweet but have a strong flavour of beetroot. Sharpen with a few drops of vinegar, or lemon juice, salt and sugar. The addition of these last two gives a piquant flavour. Then strain the soup through a piece of muslin. If wished, add the consommé at this stage.

Serve the soup in cups with a bowl of soured cream handed separately, if wished. Serve the hot pirozhki separately.

Pirozhki

8 oz flour
1 teaspoon salt
scant ½ oz yeast
1 teaspoon sugar
3-4 tablespoons milk
2 eggs
2 oz butter

For filling

1 small onion (chopped)
1 oz butter
2 oz mushrooms (sliced), or ½ oz
  dried mushrooms
2 eggs (hard-boiled and chopped)
3 oz long grain rice (boiled until
  tender, drained and dried)
salt and pepper
beaten egg (optional) — to bind

*Placing filling for pirozhki on rounds
of dough before folding*

Method

Sift the flour with the salt into a warm bowl. Work the yeast with the sugar, then add the milk, warmed to blood heat. Whisk the eggs and add to the flour with the yeast mixture, beating well with your hand. The dough should be rather soft, a little more so than for a scone dough. Then cream the butter, add to the dough and cover the basin with a plate. Leave in the refrigerator overnight; at the end of this time the dough should have risen to the top of the basin and will be firm enough to handle easily.

To make the filling: soften the onion in a pan with the butter, add the mushrooms and cook briskly for 2-3 minutes; turn into a bowl and mix with eggs and rice. Season well. If wished, this mixture may be bound with a little beaten egg for easy handling.

Roll out the dough and stamp it out into rounds about 2½ inches in diameter: put a spoonful of the filling in the centre of each round, and brush with beaten egg; bring the edges up over the top and pinch well together. Prove in a warm place for 7-10 minutes and, when lightly risen, fry in deep fat on a rising temperature to allow pies to cook through without overbrowning the surface. If preferred they may be fried some time before they are wanted, then put into a hot oven for 4-5 minutes to heat them through. Alternatively, brush with beaten egg and bake in a hot oven (400°F or Mark 6).

Though these are good baked they are nicer deep fat fried.

Chicken and pineapple rice

2 roasting, or boiling, chickens
(each weighing 3½ lb dressed)
flavouring vegetables and herbs
(for poaching)
1 lb long grain rice
good pinch of saffron (soaked in
2-3 tablespoons warm
water) — optional
3 oz butter
3 medium-size onions (thinly sliced)
2-3 oz blanched almonds (well
soaked, then split and shredded)
1 good-size fresh pineapple, or 1
can pineapple slices
2 oranges
1-2 tablespoons sugar
4 eggs (hard-boiled and sliced)
small carton (2½ fl oz) of cream —
optional

The stock obtained from poaching the chickens may be used for cooking the rice or for the bortschok (page 44), in place of water.

Method

Poach the chickens in water barely to cover, with a bunch of herbs and vegetables to flavour, until tender (45-50 minutes for roasting chickens, 2-3 hours for boiling chickens). Cool chicken in the liquid, then take out and skin; cut off the flesh neatly and slice it into shreds.

Boil the rice in stock or water, with the saffron, if used, until tender (about 12 minutes). Strain and drain thoroughly. If using water, rinse as usual; with stock this is unnecessary as the small amount of fat in the stock helps to keep grains separate, and rinsing would wash away flavour of the stock.

Melt half the butter, add the onions, cook slowly for 3-4 minutes, then add almonds (well drained) and continue to cook slowly, stirring with a fork, until coloured to a light brown. Set aside.

Peel, slice and core the pineapple (or, if using a can, drain off the syrup); slice each ring through, then cut in half. Slice the oranges thinly, leaving on the peel. Melt the rest of the butter in a large frying pan, put in the orange slices, then dust well with sugar and fry quickly on both sides until brown. Take out orange slices and add the pineapple; turn the pieces around and shake the pan for a few minutes over brisk heat.

Layer the rice, chicken and hard-boiled eggs in a well buttered ovenproof dish with the onions, almonds and about half the pineapple. Pile the mixture up well, then surround with the orange rings, overlapping, and the rest of the pineapple. Cover with buttered paper, or foil, and set aside for reheating, or keep in a warm oven.

Watchpoint If, when reheating, the rice is a little dry, pour over the cream.

Pheasant flamande

1 good brace of pheasants (or, if small, a brace plus 1)
about 3 oz butter
2 fl oz brandy
1 medium-size onion (stuck with a clove)
2-3 sticks of celery (cut in half and tied together)
$\frac{1}{4}$ pint jellied stock
about 1 teaspoon arrowroot (for thickening)
$\frac{1}{4}$ pint double cream

Serves 8 people.

Method
Heat a large pan or flameproof casserole, drop in the butter and put in the pheasants, breast side down. Brown them slowly, turning frequently (this will take about 10-15 minutes). Then heat the brandy, set it alight and flame the pheasants. Add the onion and celery, season, and cover the casserole tightly. Cook slowly on top of stove or in the oven (at 350°F or Mark 4) for about 35-40 minutes. Turn the birds once or twice during this time.

Then take up the pheasants, cut into slices and lay in an ovenproof dish. Remove the onion and celery from the pan and add the stock, thickened very lightly with a little arrowroot, then add the cream and boil rapidly for 1-2 minutes. Pour this sauce over the pheasants.

Spiced oranges

10 large sweet oranges
1 pint white wine vinegar
$2\frac{1}{2}$ lb lump sugar
4-inch stick of cinnamon
14 cloves
6 blades of mace

Serves 12 people.

These go well with cold meat. Use 2 lb screw-top jars.

Method
Cut the oranges into slices $\frac{1}{4}$ inch thick and put them in a pan with water just to cover. Put the lid half on the pan and simmer the slices until the peel is tender (about 1 hour).

Put the vinegar, sugar and spices into a preserving pan and boil for 5 minutes.

Drain the orange slices but reserve the liquor. Put about half the orange slices in the syrup and simmer gently for about 30 minutes.

Watchpoint It is most important that the orange slices are fully covered by the syrup, so it is advisable to cook them in two batches.

Lift out the cooked slices with a draining spoon into a bowl. Add the rest of the oranges to the pan and, if not covered by the remaining syrup, add a little of the reserved orange liquor. Cook as before. Turn into a bowl, cover with a plate and leave overnight.

The next morning tip off any remaining syrup and boil it until thick. Add the oranges and reboil. If the syrup is already thick, merely heat it slowly to boiling point, with the orange slices. Fill into warm dry preserving jars and cover at once.

47

Gâteau chinois à l'orange

4 oz plain flour
pinch of salt
4 eggs
6 oz caster sugar
5-6 sugar lumps
2 oranges
¾ pint double cream
2-3 tablespoons sliced glacé
  ginger

For decoration

extra double cream
extra glacé ginger, or crystallised
  orange slices.

*2-6 baking sheets and 2-6 cooling
  racks*

Serves 8 people.

Method

Prepare the baking sheets in the following way: brush with melted lard or oil, dust lightly with flour, then mark an 8-inch circle on each, using a plate or saucepan lid as a guide. Set the oven at 375°F or Mark 5.

Sift the flour with the salt. Break the eggs into a bowl, add the sugar and whisk over hot water until the mixture is thick and white (if using electric mixer, no heat is necessary). Remove from the heat and continue whisking until the bowl is cold. Fold the flour lightly into the mixture, using a metal spoon. Divide mixture into 6

portions and spread over a circle on the prepared sheets (this can be done with fewer sheets, in rotation, but each time they must be wiped, re-greased and floured). Bake in the pre-set moderate oven for about 5-8 minutes. Trim each round with a sharp knife while still on the baking sheet, then lift it on to a wire rack to cool.

Rub the sugar lumps over the oranges to remove all the zest, then pound sugar to a syrup with a little orange juice. Whip the cream and sweeten with the orange syrup. Sandwich the 6 rounds of cake with the orange cream and sliced ginger. Decorate with extra cream, and ginger or crystallised orange slices.

◀ *The finished gâteau chinois à l'orange, showing the layers of cake, cream and glacé ginger*

Hot punches and Cold cups

Wassail

2 quarts good ale
½ bottle sherry
½ teaspoon each of ground cinnamon, ginger and nutmeg
2 strips of lemon rind
8 crab apples, or 4 small red apples
soft brown sugar (to taste)

Method
Add the sherry, spices and lemon rind to $1\frac{3}{4}$ quarts of the ale and heat, then simmer for 5 minutes. Bake the apples until just soft with the sugar and baste with remaining ale. Add these to the spiced ale, adding more sugar if necessary. Serve hissing hot in tankards.

Bishop

1 bottle of port
1 orange (stuck with 6 cloves)
sugar (to taste)

Bishop is the name given by Oxford and Cambridge under-graduates to mulled port and it is served from a punch bowl. In Northern Europe 'Bischof' re-fers to any hot, spiced wine.

Method
Cut the orange in half and put it in a stainless steel, or tin-lined copper, pan with the port and a little sugar (some people prefer it without). Heat gently and when at simmering point set alight and allow it to burn for some seconds, then pour into a warmed punch bowl. Serve with a ladle.
Note : if wished bishop may be diluted with a little water, about $\frac{1}{2}$ pint to the above quantity.

▶ 49

Hot punches and Cold cups continued

Claret punch

2 bottles of claret
1 orange
1 lemon (thickly sliced and
   stuck with 6 cloves)
1 3-inch stick of cinnamon
12 sugar lumps
4 fl oz brandy

Method

Bake orange for 30 minutes at 375°F or Mark 5. Turn claret into a scrupulously clean saucepan (stainless steel or tin-lined copper), add the lemon, cinnamon, baked orange and half the sugar. Set on low heat and keep at simmering point for 15 minutes with the pan uncovered. Then turn the contents into a punch bowl and remove the cinnamon. (If using a glass bowl, first cool punch a little.) Put brandy into a small pan with rest of the sugar, heat slowly to dissolve the sugar, then set light to the brandy; leave for a few seconds then pour into the punch bowl.

Whisky punch

1 bottle of whisky
thinly pared rind and strained
   juice of 2 large lemons
½ lb lump sugar
3 pints boiling water

Method

Put the rind and juice of the lemons with the sugar into a punch bowl. Pour on the boiling water, stir until the sugar is dissolved, then add the whisky. Stir well and serve with a ladle.

Hot cider punch

2 quarts dry, or medium dry,
   cider (according to taste)
3 fl oz brandy
2 oranges (each stuck with 6
   cloves)
2 dessert apples (sliced)
sugar (to taste)

Method

Turn the cider into a large pan and add the other ingredients. Simmer for 20-30 minutes, then pour into punch bowl.

Champagne cup

1 bottle of Champagne
1½ fl oz orange curaçao
4 fl oz brandy
little icing sugar
about ¾ pint soda water
good dash of Angostura bitters
small quantity of fruit in season
grapes, etc.
2-3 sprigs of borage, or mint
   (bruised)
few ice cubes

Method

Chill the Champagne well before opening. Mix it with the curaçao and brandy and sweeten with a little icing sugar before adding soda and remaining ingredients.

Hock cup

2 bottles of hock
1½ fl oz orange curaçao
4 fl oz brandy
good dash of Angostura bitters
about ½ pint soda water
small quantity of fruit in season
(sliced) — eg. pineapple, orange,
grapes, etc.
2-3 sprigs of borage, or mint
(bruised)
few ice cubes

Method
Mix all ingredients (except the ice) about one hour before serving. Add ice just before serving.

Claret cup

2 bottles of claret
2½ fl oz brandy
1½ fl oz orange curaçao
1 orange (sliced)
1 rounded tablespoon sugar
about 1 pint soda water
2-3 sprigs of borage, or lemon
verbena
2-3 strips of cucumber
about 1 teaspoon Angostura bitters

Method
Mix all ingredients together in a large jug, leaving the soda to the last (this is usually added before serving). Chill lightly rather than add ice cubes.

▲

Preparing good coffee

Put coffee in a warm earthenware jug with a tiny pinch of salt; then stand jug in a warm place.

When coffee is warmed through, pour on boiling water and stir well with a wooden spoon. Cover jug with a saucer and leave in a warm place for 10-15 minutes. Splash in a few drops of cold water to settle the grounds and stand again for 2-3 minutes; then strain carefully.

Just before starting meal, place coffee in a clean hot pot and leave standing in a deep pan of hot water just below simmering point. When ready to serve, hand the hot milk separately.

Café brûlot

1½ pints strong black coffee
5-6 fl oz brandy
6 sugar lumps (rubbed into the rind of 1 tangerine)
1 stick of cinnamon (broken in half)
4-5 cloves

Method
Put the sugar, brandy, cinnamon and cloves into a scrupulously clean saucepan (stainless steel, or tin-lined copper). Heat slowly, then set light to the brandy and let it burn out. Pour on the very hot coffee, stir round, then ladle into warm coffee cups.

Gaelic coffee

Irish whiskey
hot, strong, black coffee
double cream
brown sugar - optional

Method
Warm large coffee cups, or glasses, and pour a tot of whiskey into each. Fill up with scalding hot coffee (adding brown sugar, if required), then pour 1 tablespoon of the cream on to the surface of the coffee over the back of a spoon. Serve at once without stirring.

Twelfth Night

We are giving here some suggestions for Twelfth Night parties, designed to serve 16 people. A white wine could be served, but always offer a soft drink or water for those who prefer it. Coffee should be served afterwards.

Turkey en gelée

10-12 lb turkey
1 medium-size onion (stuck with a
   clove)
3 oz butter
$\frac{1}{4}$ pint stock
1 glass sherry

For mousse
1$\frac{1}{2}$ lb cooked ham
$\frac{1}{2}$ lb butter (creamed)
$\frac{1}{2}$ pint béchamel sauce (made with
   1$\frac{1}{2}$ oz butter, 1$\frac{1}{2}$ oz flour and $\frac{1}{2}$ pint
   flavoured milk) - see page 9
$\frac{1}{4}$ pint double cream
$\frac{1}{2}$ lb cooked tongue (finely shredded)
salt and pepper

For garnish
2 pints aspic jelly
16 tartlet cases of shortcrust pastry
1 truffle
2 cans cranberry sauce

Method

Set the oven at 375°F or Mark
5. Place the onion and 1 oz of
the butter inside the bird, place
in a roasting tin and pour round
the stock and sherry. Melt the
remaining butter and pour it
over the turkey. Cover the bird
with greaseproof paper and
foil and cook in the pre-set
oven, allowing 15 minutes to the
pound and 15 minutes over.
Leave the turkey to cool.
   Prepare the aspic jelly (see
page 9) and make the rich shortcrust pastry and set aside to
chill. (See pastry method page
28.) Line the pastry on to the
small tartlet tins and bake blind
(for about 8 minutes in an oven
at 375°F or Mark 5). Allow to
cool.
   To prepare the mousse : pass
the ham through the mincer

twice and then mix with the
creamed butter and cold
béchamel sauce. Partially whip
the cream and fold it into the
ham mixture with the tongue
and season well.
   Cut the wing and breast
fillets, each in one piece, from
the turkey and remove the breastbone with poultry scissors. Fill
the carcass with the mousse,
shaping it carefully with a
palette knife to simulate the
shape of the breastbone.
Carve each fillet in neat, even-
size slices and replace on the
mousse. Arrange slices of truffle
along line of removed breastbone. Baste with cold aspic
jelly and leave to set.
   Chop the remaining aspic,
place on a large serving dish
and set the turkey on top. Fill
each tartlet case with a spoonful of cranberry sauce and
arrange round the turkey.

*Below : basting the turkey with aspic
after the sliced fillets have been
replaced on the bird*

Celery and green pepper chartreuse

1 packet of lime jelly
juice of ½ temon
1 tablespoon onion juice
1 green pepper
1 cap of canned pimiento
¼ pint mayonnaise (see page 10)
4 sticks of celery (diced)
sprigs of watercress

Ring mould (2½ pints capacity)

Method

Break the jelly into cubes, pour on ½ pint boiling water, stir until dissolved, then add the lemon and onion juice, and make up to ¾ pint with cold water; leave to cool.

Folding chopped celery, pepper and pimiento into the whisked jelly and mayonnaise mixture for celery and green pepper chartreuse

Remove the core and seeds from the green pepper and cut the flesh in dice. Blanch these in boiling water for 1 minute, then drain and refresh. Dice the pimiento. When the jelly begins to thicken, whisk vigorously until it looks foamy, then fold in the mayonnaise and the prepared celery, pepper and pimiento. Pour into the mould, cover and leave to set.

When ready to serve, dip the mould quickly in and out of hot water, turn jelly on to a serving platter and garnish with sprigs of watercress.

Garnishing the finished celery and green pepper chartreuse with sprigs of watercress

Gratin florentine

1 lb frozen leaf spinach
$\frac{1}{4}$ pint milk
4 eggs (beaten)
4 egg yolks (beaten)
salt
pepper (ground from mill)
$\frac{1}{4}$ pint single cream
little nutmeg (freshly grated)
8 oz long grain rice (cooked)
4 oz Cheddar cheese (grated)
1 oz Parmesan cheese (grated)

Method
Allow the spinach to thaw, press between 2 plates to remove the excess moisture, then chop finely. Set the oven at 375°F or Mark 5. Heat the milk, tip it on to the beaten eggs and yolks, season well and add the cream and nutmeg.

Butter an ovenproof dish and fill with layers of spinach, rice and Cheddar cheese, beginning and ending with spinach; pour over the egg mixture. Mix any remaining Cheddar cheese with the Parmesan and sprinkle this over the top. Cook au bain-marie (see page 9) in the pre-set oven till brown and crisp on the top, about 30 minutes.

Salade de saison

2 Webb's lettuces
3 avocado pears

For dressing
3 tablespoons white wine vinegar
salt and pepper
6 tablespoons salad oil
1 tablespoon poppy seeds

Method
Wash and dry the lettuce very well and break into bite-size pieces. This is best done with the fingers. Prepare the dressing in the usual way, adding the poppy seeds when the dressing is emulsified. Pour over the lettuce and mix well. Peel the avocados, cut into thin slices and add to the lettuce. Toss once again, but avoid breaking the avocados. Tip into a large salad bowl.

Sandwiches

The following selection of sandwiches are made with either rye, white, brown or pumpernickel (Westphalian brown) bread, but whatever bread is chosen. Remember that the thickness of filling should be at least twice that of the bread. The bread should, of course, be fresh and, if preferred, the crusts can be removed.

When preparing sandwiches for a large party it is always worth inquiring from the bakers to see whether they will slice the bread extra thin but if you are slicing the bread yourself remember it is always easier to cut the bread if it is buttered first. Each round of sandwiches should be cut into four; allow at least 2 rounds per person.

Accompaniments should be arranged in separate dishes so the guests can help themselves to a selection just as they like. A fruit cup, wine cup, beer or lager can be served with the sandwiches.

Salted brisket sandwich

Take light rye bread, butter and spread with French mustard. Cover with a $\frac{1}{4}$-inch layer of crisp shredded lettuce, bound with a little mayonnaise, and cover this with the thinly cut salted brisket which should be at least 4 layers thick. Cover with a second layer of buttered bread.

Ham and cream cheese sandwich

Take dark rye bread, butter and spread with a very thin layer of English mustard. Then spread with a $\frac{1}{4}$-inch layer of cream cheese, well seasoned with celery salt. Cover this with 2-3 layers of sliced ham and then with a second slice of buttered bread.

Cream cheese and pineapple sandwich

Butter wholemeal bread and cover each slice with a $\frac{1}{2}$-inch layer of cream cheese and cover the bottom slice with chopped watercress. Place a slice of fresh pineapple, cut into bite-size pieces, on top of watercress and top with second slice of bread and cheese.

Roast beef sandwich

Butter white bread, cover with a $\frac{1}{4}$-inch layer of grated cooked beetroot mixed with a little horseradish cream. Cover this with layers of very thinly sliced cold roast beef, sprinkle with salt and cover with a second layer of buttered white bread.

Crab sandwich

Use frozen or canned white crab meat, flake and mix with mayonnaise. Butter some wholemeal bread and cover with a thick layer of the crab. Cover this with sliced cucumber and a second layer of crab. Top with a slice of buttered bread. ▶

Sandwiches continued

Prawn sandwich

Butter wholemeal bread and to every $\frac{1}{2}$ pound of prawns take 3 sticks of celery (chopped), and one sharp dessert apple (peeled, cored and chopped). Bind with 1 tablespoon of tomato chutney and 3 tablespoons of mayonnaise. Mix the prawns into this and sandwich between the buttered bread.

Liver sausage and chutney sandwich

Take white bread, butter and spread it with French mustard and then cover with a $\frac{1}{4}$-inch layer of shredded lettuce mixed with a little mayonnaise. Cover this with a layer of liver sausage cut into dice (this is best done with a knife dipped in hot water) and lightly tossed with a little chutney of your choice. Finish with a second layer of buttered white bread.

Tongue sandwich

Take rye bread with caraway seeds, spread with unsalted butter and then with some hot mustard. Cover with a layer of shredded crisp lettuce and top with about 3 slices of tongue. Top with another slice of buttered bread.

Mortadella open sandwich

Spread thinly sliced pumpernickel with unsalted butter, cover with finely sliced Dutch cheese such as Edam or Samso. Cover the cheese with sliced mortadella and serve open with a garnish of sliced stuffed olives.

Salami open sandwich

Spread sliced pumpernickel with unsalted butter and then with a thin coating of the following mixture. Chop 1 cap of canned pimiento and one large dill cucumber and moisten with enough mayonnaise to bind it together. Cover with thinly sliced salami and serve open, decorated with a pickled walnut or a black olive.

Chicken and bacon toasted sandwich

Toast thin slices of white bread on one side only and butter the untoasted side well. While still hot cover with sliced chicken, moistened with mayonnaise. Top with 3-4 rashers of streaky bacon cut at No. 4 and grilled until crisp. Top with another slice of toast, buttered on the untoasted side.

Good at an informal party : toasted chicken and bacon sandwich

Kipper pâté

3-4 kippers (according to size)
8 oz cream cheese
good pinch of paprika pepper
pepper (ground from mill)
salt (optional)
1-2 tablespoons single cream, or
   creamy milk

Method

Poach the kippers in water for 5-6 minutes and cool slightly in the liquid, then remove the skin and bones. Weigh the flesh — it should weigh 12 oz.

Work the cheese to a smooth cream, adding the paprika and pepper and, if necessary, a little salt. Add the cream (or creamy milk). Pound the kipper flesh, then gradually work it into the cheese. (This could be done by an electric mixer.) Adjust the seasoning and when pâté is soft and light pile it into a dish for serving with water biscuits.

Savoury flan with relishes

For rich shortcrust pastry

8 oz plain flour
5 oz butter
1 oz lard
1 egg yolk
about 3-4 tablespoons water

For filling

1 lb minced beef
1-2 tablespoons good dripping, or oil
1 onion (finely chopped)
1 rounded tablespoon flour
$\frac{1}{4}$ pint stock, or water
salt and pepper
Worcestershire sauce (to taste)
1 lb potatoes
little hot milk
$\frac{1}{2}$ oz butter
1 egg yolk (optional)

8-9 inch diameter flan ring

Two flans will serve 16 people.

Method

First prepare the pastry (see page 28), chill and then roll out and line into the flan ring. Prick the bottom and bake blind. Meanwhile heat the dripping (or oil) in a frying pan or flameproof casserole. Put in the onion and after 3-4 minutes add the mince. Cook for 2-3 minutes, stirring well. When the mixture is turning colour, draw aside and stir in flour and liquid. Season and stir until boiling.

Cover and simmer gently for about 1-1$\frac{1}{2}$ hours until the mince is really tender. The mixture should be the consistency of thick cream. (It may be necessary to add a little more liquid as the mince cooks.) Add the Worcestershire sauce.

Meanwhile boil the potatoes until tender, drain and dry.

Crush well or put through a Mouli sieve and beat to a fairly firm purée with hot milk, butter and egg yolk (if using).

Fill the flan case to within one-eighth of an inch of the top with the mince mixture and pipe the potato round the edge and across in lattice fashion. Brown flan in oven at 425°F or Mark 7 for about 15 minutes. Serve hot with these relishes.

Beetroot relish

2 large cooked beetroots
2 tart dessert, or cooking, apples
3-4 tablespoons French dressing (see page 40) with a little garlic added

Method

Grate the beetroot coarsely; peel, quater and core the apples and cut into dice. Mix with the beetroot and moisten with a little of the French dressing. Pile into a dish for serving.

Celery and cheese relish

1 head of celery
1-2 green peppers
4-6 oz mild Cheddar, or Gouda, cheese (diced)
French dressing (see page 40)

Method

Clean the celery and chop coarsely. Chop and blanch the peppers, drain and mix with the celery. Add the cheese and moisten with French dressing. Pile into a dish for serving.

Onion relish

2 Spanish onions
4-6 oz mushrooms
squeeze of lemon juice
salt and pepper
French dressing (see page 40)
1 dessertspoon chopped parsley
  (optional)

Method

Cut the onions into slices and push out into rings. Put the rings into cold water, bring to the boil, drain and then repeat this process and simmer until barely cooked. Drain thoroughly.

Meanwhile slice the mushrooms thickly and barely cook with a little water and the lemon juice; season. Drain and mix with the onion. Moisten with a little French dressing and add the chopped parsley, if liked. Pile into dish for serving.

Tomato and anchovy relish

about $\frac{3}{4}$ lb tomatoes
about 1 dessertspoon anchovy
  essence
1 tablespoon vinegar
3 tablespoons oil
1 tablespoon double cream
pepper (ground from mill)

Method

Skin and quarter tomatoes; remove seeds. Combine all the liquid ingredients to make a dressing and season well with pepper. Add dressing to tomatoes and pile into a dish for serving.

Savoury flan and relishes — tomato and anchovy, onion, celery and cheese, beetroot

Gâteau lyonnais au chocolat

4 oz plain flour
pinch of salt
4 oz butter
8 eggs
12 oz caster sugar
3-4 drops of vanilla essence
1 lb chestnuts (boiled, skinned and
    sieved)
¾ pint double cream
4 oz dessert chocolate
2 tablespoons water
1 dessertspoon caster sugar
6 tablespoons orange jelly
    marmalade

For chocolate glacé icing
6 oz plain block chocolate
6-8 tablespoons stock syrup (see
    page 10), or water
1 lb icing sugar (finely sieved)
1 teaspoon salad oil
2-3 drops of vanilla essence

Three 9-inch diameter sandwich tins

The region around Lyons, in
France, is famous for its sweet
chestnuts.

*Above : sandwiching three layers of
gâteau lyonnais with chocolate flavoured cream*
*Below : pouring slightly warm choco-
late glacé icing over gâteau lyonnais
au chocolat*

Method

Set oven at 375°F or Mark 5.
Prepare the cake tins by brushing with melted fat. Put a disc
of paper in the bottom of each
tin, grease this, and then dust
tins with flour and sugar.

Sift the flour with salt. Melt
the butter very gently, taking
care that it does not oil.
Whisk the eggs, add the sugar
and vanilla essence and continue whisking until mixture
will form a ribbon on itself. This
can be done with an electric
mixer, or by hand in a bowl
over a pan of hot water.

When the egg and sugar
mixture is very thick, fold in the
prepared chestnuts, then the

sifted flour and last of all the
prepared butter. Divide mixture
evenly between the prepared
tins and bake in pre-set oven
for about 30 minutes. Turn
the cakes on to a rack to cool.

Whip the cream until thick
and divide into two portions
with two-fifths in one bowl
and three-fifths in the other.
Melt the chocolate in the water
and allow to cool, add this to
the smaller portion of cream;

add the sugar to other bowl.

When the cakes are quite cold, split them, spread each of the six layers with a thin layer of the orange jelly marmalade and cover with a good layer of the plain sweetened cream. Reshape the three cakes and sandwich them with the chocolate cream. To prepare the chocolate glacé icing: cut the chocolate into small pieces and put them in a saucepan with the stock syrup (or water). Dissolve the chocolate over gentle heat and then bring just to the boil. Allow to cool before beating in sugar, 1 spoonful at a time. Add oil and vanilla and warm slightly before pouring over cake.

Below : a slice of gâteau lyonnais, showing layers of cake, cream, and chocolate cream

Upside-down apple tart

1 lb cooking apples (peeled, cored and thinly sliced)
2 oz butter
4 tablespoons granulated sugar
$\frac{1}{2}$ lb quantity of puff pastry (see page 10)

To serve
$\frac{1}{2}$ pint double cream (whipped)

Method
Set the oven at 350°F or Mark 4. Put the butter, apples and sugar into a round ovenproof dish. Cook in the pre-set moderate oven for about 30 minutes until the apples are barely done.

Remove dish from oven and then turn the heat up to 425-450°F or Mark 7-8. Roll the pastry and cover the dish; put it back into the oven for 12-15 minutes. Take out and turn upside-down on to a serving dish. Serve immediately with whipped cream.

Fresh fruit jelly

6 clementines
4 ripe dessert pears
1 lb black, or white, grapes
1$\frac{1}{2}$ lb sugar lumps
3 pints water
finely pared rind and juice of 3 lemons
4$\frac{1}{2}$ oz gelatine (soaked in 14 fl oz water)
3 cans (6$\frac{1}{4}$ fl oz each) concentrated frozen orange juice (made up with 2 pints water)

Method
Put the sugar and water in a pan with the lemon rind and juice. Dissolve over gentle heat, then simmer for 5 minutes. Strain this syrup through muslin, wringing it out very well to remove all the syrup and essence from the lemon rind. Add the soaked gelatine to the hot syrup and stir until completely dissolved.

Watchpoint It is important to have the gelatine soaking in the cold water before the sugar syrup is prepared. It should be added to the hot syrup as soon as this has been strained.

Add the diluted orange juice to the sugar syrup and gelatine mixture and allow to cool.

Peel and slice the clementines; peel, core and slice the ripe pears; skin and pip the grapes. Arrange the fruit in a glass bowl and pour on cool jelly. Cover and allow to set.

Serve a bowl of whipped cream with the jelly.

Easter

In the following pages we cover your Easter holiday cooking :
time-saving meals for Good Friday, a dinner party for
Saturday, a Sunday evening Buffet and a picnic for Monday
as well as how to make traditional hot cross buns and
decorate your Easter eggs.

Hot cross buns

1 lb plain flour
$\frac{1}{2}$ teaspoon salt
$\frac{1}{2}$ teaspoon mixed spice
scant $\frac{1}{2}$ pint milk
$\frac{3}{4}$ oz yeast (fresh, or dried)
2-4 oz butter
2 oz caster sugar
2 eggs (beaten)
6 oz currants (cleaned)
1 oz candied peel (finely chopped) —
   optional
little extra flour (for dusting)
sweetened milk (for finishing)

Nowadays these buns are made individually but they were originally baked as one large bun. This quantity makes about 16 buns.

Method

Sift the flour with salt and mixed spice into a bowl. Warm the milk carefully to blood heat (98°F) and add the yeast and butter. Stir until yeast is dissolved, then mix in the sugar and eggs. Make a well in the flour, tip in the liquid ingredients and beat until smooth.

Turn dough on to a floured board, work in the currants and candied peel. Knead dough until it is elastic, then place it in a warmed, greased bowl. Sprinkle the dough with extra flour and cover with a clean tea towel.

Set dough to rise in a warm place for $1\frac{1}{2}$ hours, or until it is doubled in bulk, then knock down dough and leave to rise again for another 30 minutes. Set oven at 425°F or Mark 7.

Shape the dough into small, round buns; with the back of a knife, mark each one with a cross on the top. Arrange the buns on a greased baking sheet and leave to prove until they are nearly twice their size. This should not take more than about 15 minutes.

Note : strips of shortcrust pastry or a special flour and water paste may be used to make the crosses.

Brush bun tops with a little sweetened milk and bake them in pre-set oven for 15 minutes.

Note : a steamy atmosphere in the oven is best for baking buns; this can be obtained by placing a roasting tin of boiling water at the bottom of the oven.

Leave buns to cool; when cold put them in a polythene bag and store in the bread bin.

Cod au gratin

1½ lb cod fillet, or frozen cod steaks
salt and pepper
1 tablespoon grated cheese
1 tablespoon brown crumbs
1 tablespoon butter (melted)

For béchamel sauce
½ pint milk
1 slice of onion
½ bayleaf
1 blade of mace
6 peppercorns
1 oz butter
1 oz flour

To save time in the preparation and cooking we would serve frozen spinach, either leaf or purée, with this dish. Creamed potatoes could be cooked and completed in the time it takes to bake the fish.

Method

Skin, wash and dry the fillet and place it on a plate. If using frozen cod steaks, allow them to thaw slowly. Dust cod lightly with salt and leave for 30 minutes.

To prepare béchamel sauce: scald the milk in a pan with the onion, bayleaf, mace and peppercorns, infuse for 10 minutes, then strain and reserve.

Melt the butter, draw pan aside and blend in the flour and flavoured milk; season with salt, stir over gentle heat until boiling, then simmer for 2-3 minutes. Taste for seasoning. Tip sauce into a basin, cover with buttered paper to prevent a skin forming, leave to cool.

Tip away any liquid that has run from the fish, pat it dry with absorbent paper, then cut in even-size pieces; put these into a buttered ovenproof dish. Set oven at 375°F or Mark 5. Spoon the cold sauce over the fish and dust with the cheese and crumbs mixed together; sprinkle with the melted butter and bake in pre-set oven for 25-30 minutes.

Watchpoint It is important that the fish should cover the bottom of the dish, then any cooking juices will blend with the white sauce. The brown crumbs mixed with the cheese give fish a good crisp coating when baked and prevent any 'pools' of fat forming on the top, which might happen if cheese only is used.

Pears Cassis

4-6 ripe dessert pears (2 over for second helpings)
6 tablespoons granulated sugar
$\frac{1}{2}$ pint water
1 vanilla pod, or 2-3 drops of vanilla essence
1 small can blackcurrants (about 7$\frac{1}{2}$ fl oz)
1 dessertspoon arrowroot
caster sugar (for dusting)

Method

Dissolve the sugar in pan of water, add the vanilla pod, boil for 5 minutes, then draw aside; if using vanilla essence, add it at this stage.

Peel and halve the pears, scoop out the core with the point of a teaspoon and put pears straight into the pan of syrup, rounded side down. Bring syrup to the boil, letting it boil right up and over the fruit, then lower the heat. Cover the pan and leave pears to simmer very gently until they look almost transparent. Leave them to cool in the covered pan. Rub the blackcurrants through a fine strainer or work to a purée in a liquidiser, measure and make quantity up to $\frac{3}{4}$ pint with syrup from the pears; then tip into a pan and heat gently.

Mix the arrowroot with 2 tablespoons pear syrup, add to the blackcurrant mixture and stir until boiling.

Drain pears, put into a serving dish and pour over blackcurrant sauce, dust the top with caster sugar to prevent a skin forming and leave to cool.

Crème normande

1 large mild onion (chopped)
1 oz butter
1 tablespoon curry powder
2 dessert apples
1 dessertspoon flour
1$\frac{1}{2}$ pints chicken stock
1 dessertspoon cornflour
$\frac{1}{4}$ pint double cream
2 egg yolks
salt and pepper
lemon juice
watercress (to garnish)

Method

Soften the onions in the butter without colouring. Add curry powder and one apple, peeled, cored and sliced. After a few minutes stir in the flour. Cook for 1 minute, then pour on the stock and add the cornflour, first slaking it with a little of the stock. Bring to the boil and simmer for 5 minutes, than add cream mixed with the egg yolks. Reheat to thicken without boiling, then put the soup through a fine sieve or blender. Season and chill.

Peel and dice the remaining apple, mix with a little lemon juice and add to the soup just before serving. Garnish with watercress leaves.

Egg and mushroom, or prawn, bouchées

8 oz quantity of puff pastry (see page 10)

egg wash (made with 1 egg beaten with ½ teaspoon salt)

For filling

¼ lb mushrooms (quartered, or sliced) and 4 eggs (hard-bolled and coarsely chopped), or 4-6 oz prawns (shelled and chopped)

1½ oz butter

1 rounded tablespoon flour

½ pint milk (infused with 1 slice of onion, ½ bayleaf, 6 peppercorns)

salt and pepper

2½-inch diameter fluted cutter, 1½-inch diameter cutter (fluted, or plain)

The bouchée cases can be made the same day or a few days beforehand and stored in an airtight container. This filling is sufficient for 6-8 bouchées.

Method

Set oven at 425°F or Mark 7. Roll out made pastry to just over ¼ inch thickness and stamp it out into bouchées 2½ inches in diameter. Set on a dampened baking sheet and brush with egg wash. Make circular incisions with the smaller cutter to form lids. Bake in pre-set oven for 15-20 minutes until golden-brown.

If using eggs and mushrooms, continue as follows: trim mushrooms, wash them quickly, drain and quarter or slice them depending on their size. Melt half the butter, add the mushrooms and sauté them for 2-3 minutes. Draw pan off the heat and add the remaining butter (the heat of the pan will melt it automatically) and blend in the flour and strained, flavoured milk. Season and stir sauce until boiling; cook for 2-3 minutes, then add the eggs.

If using prawns, make sauce with butter, flour and drained milk. Stir in prawns.

Remove lids and fill bouchées with the mixture. Replace lids and reheat a few minutes in oven before serving very hot.

If you have baked bouchées a few days before, the best way to reheat them is as follows: first set oven at 350°F or Mark 4. Fill cold bouchées with hot filling and heat for 10 minutes.

Hot boiled gammon

2 lb middle cut of gammon
8 even-size carrots
4 even-size onions
6 peppercorns
1 bayleaf

By cooking whole onions and carrots in with the ham and serving them arranged round the joint, you will need only one other vegetable and we suggest potatoes in white sauce.

Method
Cover the joint with cold water, bring it slowly to the boil and then skim well. Add onions, carrots and seasonings, cover and simmer for $1\frac{1}{2}$ hours (that is about 20 minutes per lb and 20 minutes over). Leave the gammon to stand in the liquid at least 15 minutes before skinning and carving. (Reserve liquid and keep in a covered container in refrigerator for use with Sunday's buffet party soup ; likewise keep any leftover vegetables.)
Drain the vegetables and arrange them around carved gammon on the serving dish.

Potatoes in white sauce

1 large can new potatoes (about 1 lb 3 oz)
parsley (chopped)

For white sauce
$1\frac{1}{2}$ oz butter
$1\frac{1}{4}$ oz flour
$\frac{3}{4}$ pint milk
salt and pepper

Canned new potatoes will save time and labour in the kitchen. They are delicious with hot ham served in a white sauce with chopped parsley.

Method
Prepare white sauce by first making a roux, blending in the milk and seasoning. Drain the potatoes, add them to the sauce and heat carefully without boiling ; then add the parsley and serve.
Note : to save time we would put the previously made white sauce into a double saucepan for reheating and then add potatoes when the sauce is hot. In this way there would be no danger of the potatoes boiling. (We mention this point as instructions on cans of new potatoes, always say reheat without boiling.) Add the chopped parsley just before turning the potatoes into the serving dish.

Tarte aux pruneaux (Prune flan)

$\frac{3}{4}$ lb prunes
$\frac{1}{4}$ pint red wine (Burgundy, or Claret)
3 tablespoons redcurrant jelly

For almond pastry
6 oz flour
4 oz butter
1½ oz ground almonds
1½ oz caster sugar
1 egg yolk
1-2 tablespoons cold water

For custard cream
1 rounded tablespoon custard powder
$\frac{1}{4}$ pint milk
$\frac{1}{4}$ pint double cream (whipped)
1 teaspoon caster sugar

For almond filling
2 oz ground almonds
1½ tablespoons caster sugar
$\frac{1}{2}$ egg white (beaten)

7-8 inch diameter flan ring

Method

Soak prunes in wine for 2-3 hours. Prepare pastry as for shortcrust, adding almonds and sugar after rubbing in fat and before mixing with egg yolk and water. Chill pastry in refrigerator for 30 minutes. Roll out and line into flan ring; bake blind.

Simmer the prunes in the wine until tender.

Watchpoint Prunes must be cooked very gently and in a pan with a tight-fitting lid because there is so little liquid.

Lift prunes from pan with a draining spoon and set aside to cool. Add redcurrant jelly to pan and set on a low heat to melt. Whisk, if necessary, to get glaze smooth, then strain.

Put custard powder in a small pan, mix to a smooth paste with milk and stir over a gentle heat until boiling; tip into a basin and whisk well. When quite cold, whip cream, sweeten with sugar, fold into custard.

Cut prunes carefully down one side and remove stones.

To prepare almond filling: combine ground almonds and sugar, adding just enough egg white to bind mixture together and fill this into the prunes.

Spoon the custard cream into flan case, spreading it evenly. Arrange filled prunes over top to cover cream. Brush or spoon glaze over the flan.

Step-by-step to this tarte aux pruneaux (it's a long way from nursery prunes and custard!)
1 Remove stones and fill prunes neatly with the almond mixture
2 Pour the custard cream into the flan case, spreading it evenly
3 Arrange the prunes on top to cover the cream completely
4 Spoon on the cooled redcurrant glaze and then leave it to set

Roast stuffed turkey

8 lb turkey (dressed)
3-4 oz butter, or bacon fat (for roasting)
1 pint stock (made from giblets)
1 rounded tablespoon flour (for gravy)

For stuffing
1 medium-size onion (finely chopped)
2 oz butter
1 lb pork (minced)
1 cup breadcrumbs
salt and pepper
1 teaspoon dried sage
$\frac{1}{2}$ teaspoon mixed dried herbs
1 tablespoon chopped parsley
2-3 tablespoons stock, or water

Trussing needle and fine string

Method

First prepare stuffing: blanch onion by putting it in pan of cold water and bringing to the boil for 5 minutes; drain, refresh and return to the pan with butter. Cover pan with buttered paper and lid and cook onion slowly for about 5 minutes until it is golden-brown; allow to cool.

Mix the pork, breadcrumbs, seasoning and herbs together with a fork, then add the onion. Work in the stock or water a little at a time.

Set oven at 350°F or Mark 4. Stuff the turkey at the neck end (you should also have enough stuffing for the body cavity because you do not want this stuffing to bulge out too much or it might get dry and over-cooked).

Watchpoint Do not stuff the turkey until the day it is to be cooked.

Pull flap of neck skin gently over stuffing and fasten under the wing tips with a skewer. Then truss the bird.

Put turkey into a roasting tin, spread butter or bacon fat over a double sheet of greaseproof paper or sheet of foil; lay this over the bird and pour round half the stock. Cook in pre-set oven, allowing 15 minutes per lb and 15 minutes over. Turn and baste bird every 20 minutes but keep paper or foil on while cooking.

If stock reduces too much during cooking, add a little more. After 1 hour cut trussing string holding the legs. To test if the bird is cooked pierce thigh with a skewer; if clear juice runs out, the bird is ready. If bird is not brown enough towards end of cooking time, remove paper and leave bird until golden-brown.

Once cooked, set bird on a serving dish, pull out trussing string and skewers. Keep the turkey warm.

To make gravy: strain juices from roasting tin into a pan and deglaze tin with remaining stock. Add this to juices in pan and skim off some of the fat. Put fat back into tin, stir in flour, then liquid from pan; stir until boiling. Season and strain gravy back into pan. When ready to serve turkey, reheat gravy and serve it separately.

Almond and raisin pilaf

2 oz butter
1 small onion (chopped)
8 oz long grain rice
1¼ - 1½ pints chicken stock
salt and pepper
2 oz raisins
2 oz almonds (shredded)
  (see page 9)
1 bayleaf

Method

Set oven at 375°F or Mark 5.

Melt 1½ oz butter in a large flameproof casserole, add the onion and cook it slowly until soft and golden; add the rice and cook for 3 minutes.

Pour on 1¼ pints chicken stock, bring to the boil, season to taste, add the raisins and almonds and mix in with a fork. Put the bayleaf on top, cover casserole and cook in the pre-set oven for 20 minutes.

Test the rice; if cooked and tender, dot the remaining butter over the top, cover casserole and leave on top of the stove until wanted. If rice is not quite tender, add remaining stock and return casserole to the oven for 5-8 minutes. Then dot the remaining butter on top.

Remove the bayleaf, stir rice lightly with a fork and serve.

> As a starter for this meal, we suggest a soup which can be prepared well in advance.

Bombe, or crème, favorite

8 half shells of meringue (made with 2 egg whites and 4 oz caster sugar, see page 86 — field of mushrooms)
½ pint double cream
2-3 drops of vanilla essence, or 1 tablespoon liqueur (one that marries well with the chosen fruit sauce)
1 teaspoon caster sugar

A true bombe recipe is made with layers of flavoured ice-cream frozen in a special mould, which is traditionally spherical and of copper.

This recipe is a variation using meringues and cream. It can also be made as a crème in a 1½-pints capacity charlotte tin, or 6-7 inch diameter loose-bottomed cake tin, or a spring-form mould.

This bombe does not have to be frozen but just chilled in the ice-making compartment; you do not chill a crème but pile it in a dish 30 minutes before serving.

Method

Line the bottom of your chosen mould with a disc of waxed paper and lightly oil the sides.

Break meringues into 2-3 pieces, whip cream until it just begins to thicken, flavour it with vanilla essence or liqueur and sweeten with sugar. Fold broken meringues into cream and turn at once into prepared mould or tin.

Cover mould or tin with foil, put in a polythene bag and tie securely; put in ice-making compartment or a deep-freeze for 2-3 hours (or set crème aside in a cool place). Turn out and serve with a fruit sauce.

Decorating Easter eggs

If you want to give the children a simple treat, boil their breakfast eggs in water with a few drops of different edible colourings.

To make animals or nursery rhyme characters, cut hats, long ears or silhouettes from felt, stick them on with strong adhesive; or make up your own designs with water paints (the non-toxic kind).

For very special eggs to be eaten cold, hard-boiled, or for use as table decoration, you need more ingenuity.

Select smooth-shelled white eggs. Collect primroses, primulas and, if possible, pieces of fern, which should be blanched for 1 minute in boiling water to soften them enough to adhere to the eggs.

For yellow and orange colourings use onion skins; for soft purple, fawn and grey colourings, use birch bark; red primulas give a bluish-green pattern. First pluck the flower from its stem, then wet an egg and place flowers on it to form a pattern. Hold flowers in position, cover with onion skins or birch bark, and while holding firmly, bandage tightly with 1-inch strips cut from any suitable cloth or bandage. Keep all in place with two elastic bands.

Put the egg into a pan of cold water and bring it gently to the boil, then simmer for about 15 minutes. Cool in cold water and peel off the bandage strips. The dyed eggs may then be washed before serving.

Soup of the day

1 **medium-size onion (finely chopped)**
1 **oz butter**
$\frac{1}{2}$ - $\frac{3}{4}$ **pint measure of leftover vegetables (eg. potatoes and sauce from leg of lamb or boiled gammon)**
about $\frac{1}{2}$ **pint stock (from boiled gammon)**
about $\frac{1}{2}$ **pint milk**
salt and pepper

Method
Put onion in a pan with butter, cover and cook for 4-8 minutes until soft and golden. Mix with leftover vegetables and make into purée with a Mouli sieve or in a liquidiser.

Transfer purée to a large pan, add an equal quantity of gammon stock and milk, bring to the boil, then taste for seasoning. Serve hot.

Turkey mayonnaise

white turkey meat (cut in julienne
 strips, 1½-2 inches long)
1 can consommé (about 10 fl oz)
1 dessertspoon gelatine
1 glass sherry

To decorate
3-4 gherkins
1 small jar of green olives
 (stuffed with pimiento)
5 tablespoons stock, or water
3 teaspoons gelatine
½ pint mayonnaise

*8-9 inch diameter sandwich, or deep
 cake, tin*

Method

Have enough white turkey meat
cut in julienne strips to fill a
5-inch diameter basin (not
tightly packed). Leave turkey
strips on a plate.

Heat the consommé in a pan;
soak gelatine in the sherry until
it has swelled, then add this
liquid to the consommé and
stir gently until gelatine is
dissolved; allow to cool.

Cut the gherkins in slanting
slices and cut a few olives in
neat rounds.

Sit tin in a roasting tin con-
taining 2-3 ice cubes and a little
cold water. Pour in a very thin
layer of the cold but still liquid
consommé and leave to set
before arranging your garnish
of gherkins and olives in a bold
pattern on this.

To do this quickly and well,
lift each piece of garnish with a
trussing needle (the dedicated
cook uses an old fashioned hat-
pin kept specially for the pur-
pose), dip it into the cold consommé and place garnish in
position. Now spoon over just
enough cold consommé to hold

the decoration in position. Put
in the refrigerator to set.

Then pour in more cold
consommé so that you have a
layer about ½ inch deep, return
the tin to the refrigerator or cold
larder to set.

Soak 3 teaspoons gelatine in
the stock or water for about
1 minute, then dissolve it in a
pan over gentle heat; then add
to the mayonnaise. Pour the
mayonnaise over the turkey
meat and mix together carefully;
spoon this into the prepared
tin, cover with foil and leave to
set.

To serve: dip the bottom of
the tin very quickly in and out
of a bowl of very hot water to
loosen the turkey mayonnaise;
ease it away from the sides very
quickly with a palette or round-
bladed knife.

Place the serving dish over
the top of the tin, hold firmly
and turn over; lift off the tin.
(If the tin doesn't lift off the
first time, shake it and the dish
gently from side to side — not
up and down which would
spoil the shape.)

Terrine maison

8 oz thin streaky bacon rashers
(unsmoked)

8 oz shredded raw game (hare,
rabbit, or pigeon, or lean pork,
or raw gammon rasher)

1 small wineglass sherry, or port
(optional)

1 bayleaf

$\frac{1}{4}$ pint jellied stock

luting paste (see page 103)

For farce

8 oz pigs liver (minced)

8 oz veal (minced)

8 oz fat pork (minced)

1 small onion (finely chopped)

1 dessertspoon fresh herbs
(chopped), or $\frac{1}{2}$ this quantity if
using dried herbs

salt and pepper

Method

Remove rind from bacon rashers and line them into a terrine. Work the minced meats and pork fat with the onion and herbs. Season.

Pour the wine over the shredded game and season to taste.

Put a layer (about a third) of the liver farce into the terrine or casserole. Press down well. Scatter half the shredded game on top and repeat these layers, ending with a layer of farce. Smooth the top and press on a bayleaf. Cover with lid and seal with a luting paste.

Cook in a bain-marie in the oven at 325-350°F or Mark 3-4 for $1\frac{1}{2}$-2 hours, or until firm to the touch. Remove lid, press well (using about a 4 lb weight). When cold, remove any fat round the sides and fill up with the jellied stock. Leave until quite set before turning out.

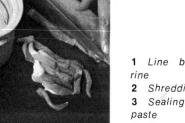

1 Line bacon rashers into terrine
2 Shredding the game
3 Sealing the lid with luting paste
4 Leave jellied stock to set before turning out

Mille feuilles

6 oz puff pastry, or trimmings (see page 10)
½ pint double cream (whipped)
3 tablespoons raspberry jam

For icing
4-6 oz icing sugar
1½ tablespoons water, or 2 of sugar syrup (made with 2 tablespoons granulated sugar dissolved in 4 tablespoons water, then boiled for 10 minutes)
2-3 drops of vanilla essence

Method

Set oven at 425°F or Mark 7.

Roll out prepared pastry as thinly as possible to a large rectangle. Lay this over dampened baking sheet, allowing pastry to come slightly over the edge. Prick pastry well all over with a fork and chill for 5-10 minutes. Then bake in pre-set oven for 10-15 minutes.

When brown in colour, slip a palette knife under pastry and turn it over. Cook in oven for a further 5 minutes, then transfer to a rack to cool. When cold, trim round edges and cut into 3 strips about 3 inches wide. Crush trimmings lightly.

Whip cream but not too stiffly. Spread one strip with half the jam, then half the cream. Lay a second strip on top and press down lightly. Spread with rest of jam and cream, top with last strip, press down again.

To make icing: mix icing sugar to a cream with water or sugar syrup, add vanilla essence. Warm icing slightly and use to coat the top. Press trimmings round edges to decorate.

Watchpoint Mille feuilles pastry must be well-baked, almost nut-brown in colour. You press layers together to prevent them moving when sliced.

Spreading the layers of pastry for mille feuilles with jam and whipped cream

Spicy tomato soup

2 lb tomatoes
1 oz butter
2 onions (finely sliced)
1 tablespoon flour
1 teaspoon paprika
1 tablespoon tomato purée
3 pints chicken, or turkey, stock
  (made from giblets)
salt and pepper
bouquet garni
1 blade of mace
1 clove
1 wineglass port

Method

Wipe the tomatoes, cut in half. Squeeze out the seeds and rub them through a nylon strainer to obtain the juice.

Melt the butter in a saucepan, add the sliced onion and cook slowly until soft but not coloured. Blend in the flour, paprika and tomato purée, then add the tomatoes and bruise well with a wooden spoon. Pour on the stock and juice from the tomato seeds, season, add the herbs and spices and stir until boiling. Simmer for 30 minutes, then strain soup.

Taste for seasoning and finally stir in the port.

Pack in wide-necked vacuum jars or flasks for easy carrying and serving.

Stuffed French loaves

Choose small French loaves (one loaf will serve three hungry people). Cut the top off each loaf, scoop out the crumb and spread the insides very thinly with butter.

Fill each loaf with a 4-egg herb (fines herbes) omelet. Slip the omelets into the loaves straight from the pan and replace the bread tops. Allow omelets to cool, then cut loaves in portions (for easy serving), push tightly together again and wrap in foil.

Herb omelet

4 eggs
1 rounded tablespoon mixed
  chopped herbs (parsley, thyme,
  marjoram or tarragon and chives)
1½ tablespoons cold water
salt
black pepper (ground from mill)
1 oz butter

7-8 inch diameter omelet pan

Method

Break eggs into a basin and beat well with a fork. When well mixed, add water, salt, pepper and herbs. Heat pan on medium heat. Put in butter in two pieces and, when frothing, pour in egg mixture at once. Leave 10-15 seconds before stirring round slowly with the flat of a fork. Do this once or twice round pan, stop and leave for another 5-6 seconds.

Lift up edge of omelet to let any remaining raw egg run on to hot pan. Now tilt pan away from you and fold over omelet to far side. Change your grip on pan so that the handle runs up the palm of your hand. Take the hot dish or plate, in your other hand, tilt it slighty and tip omelet on to it.

Devilled turkey kebabs

16 pieces of dark turkey meat
4½ tablespoons olive oil
½ teaspoon dry mustard
1 tablespoon Worcestershire sauce
2 tablespoons tomato ketchup, or similar bottled, fruity sauce
dash of Tabasco sauce
1 large green pepper (cored, deseeded, cut in squares)
12 small mushrooms
4 bayleaves
1 medium-size onion
8 rashers of streaky bacon

8 'lolly' sticks (sharpened at one end)

Method

Mix 1 teaspoon of the oil with the mustard and sauces, pour over turkey meat, and leave to marinate while preparing the other ingredients.

Cut the pepper into squares and blanch in pan of boiling water for 1 minute, then drain and refresh.

Trim the mushroom stalks level with the caps, put into a basin and pour over boiling water, leave for 1 minute, then drain. This preparation of the mushrooms helps to prevent them breaking when they are skewered.

Cut the onion in quarters and divide into segments. Cut each bayleaf in half.

Remove the rind from the bacon and cut each rasher in half, then stretch them by smoothing out with the blade of a heavy knife. Wrap each piece of devilled turkey meat in half a rasher of bacon.

Thread all the ingredients on the sharpened lolly sticks in the following order: turkey, bayleaf, onion, pepper, mushroom, pepper, turkey.

Brush the finished kebabs with remaining oil and grill until bacon is brown and crisp on all sides. When cold, wrap in greaseproof paper or foil and pack in a box.

Cut bacon rashers in half, stretch and wrap round turkey

Thread the prepared kebab items on the sharpened sticks

Brush with oil and grill until the bacon is brown and crisp. Wrap in grease-proof paper or foil and pack in box for picnic

Stuffed sausages

8 sausages
2 Demi-Sel cheeses
1 teaspoon French mustard (Dijon)
1 tablespoon tomato pickle, or chutney

Method

Work together all stuffing ingredients until firm. Grill or dry fry your favourite sausages and allow them to cool. Split sausages down one side and fill with the stuffing. Wrap in greaseproof paper or foil and pack in a box.

Sticky ginger cake

4 oz butter
4 oz soft brown sugar
2 eggs
10 oz black treacle
8 oz plain flour
pinch of salt
1 teaspoon ground ginger
4 oz sultanas (cleaned)
$\frac{1}{2}$ teaspoon bicarbonate of soda
2 tablespoons warm milk (blood heat)

8-inch diameter cake tin

This cake keeps well and can be made two weeks before it's wanted.

Method

Set oven at 325°F or Mark 3. Grease and flour tin.

Soften the butter in a bowl, add the sugar and beat thoroughly until soft; whisk in the eggs and black treacle. Sift the flour with the salt and ginger and, using a metal spoon, fold these into the mixture, with the sultanas.

Dissolve the bicarbonate of soda in the milk and carefully stir into cake mixture, pour this into the prepared tin and bake in the pre-set oven for $1\frac{1}{2}$-2 hours; after 1 hour reduce oven to 300°F or Mark 2.

Cut the cake in wedges, spread these generously with unsalted butter and top with a good slice of Gouda cheese; reshape into a cake and wrap in foil. Serve with crisp apples (Cox's Orange pippins or Golden Delicious).

Children's Birthday Party

When preparing food for a children's party don't forget that children need to have their interest stimulated. Here we give you some entertaining recipes that children will love. Portions should be small enough to be eaten quickly and leave room for the other attractive dishes.

A field of mushrooms

1 packet of lime, or greengage, jelly
$\frac{1}{4}$ pint double cream (whipped)
1 oz plain dessert chocolate (finely grated) — to decorate

For meringue
2 egg whites
4 oz caster sugar

Shallow glass bowl

Method

Prepare the jelly and when cool, pour into the bowl to set.

To make meringues : beat egg whites until stiff, whisk in 2 teaspoons of the measured sugar for 1 minute only. Fold in remaining sugar quickly and lightly with a metal spoon. Shape or pipe a number of small 'mushroom caps and stalks' on to a baking sheet lined with non-stick (siliconised) cooking paper, dust caps with grated chocolate and bake in oven for about 45 minutes at 250 - 275°F or Mark $\frac{1}{2}$-1. When cool press in underside of tops, pipe or fill in a little whipped, sweetened cream, dust with grated chocolate and fix stalks into dents. Spread any remaining cream on jelly, arrange mushrooms on top.

Orange jelly baskets

6-8 large (enough to give 1 pint juice)
3-4 lemons (depending on size)
1 pint water
8 oz lump, or granulated, sugar
rind of 2 oranges (thinly peeled)
$1\frac{1}{2}$ oz gelatine

To finish
12-14 thin strips of angelica (5 inches long)
whipped cream (optional)

Method

Halve the oranges and lemons, scoop out the flesh and press it through a strainer, or put in a blender, to remove the juice. Gently press the orange skins to flatten their base so that the halves will sit flat.

Put the water, sugar, orange rind and gelatine in a pan, stir over gentle heat until sugar and gelatine are dissolved. Cover and infuse for 10 minutes. Wring liquid through a muslin cloth and add the strained orange and lemon juice. When cool pour into the prepared orange skins and leave to set.

Dip the strips of angelica into boiling water to make them pliable and bend each into a half-circle. Before serving, fix the angelica handles over the jellies and decorate with whipped cream.

Iced chocolate biscuits

4 oz butter
2 oz caster sugar
4 oz self-raising flour
pinch of salt
1 oz sweetened chocolate
   powder

For glacé icing

1 lb icing sugar
$\frac{1}{2}$ egg white
pink and blue colouring

Method

Set oven at 375°F or Mark 5.

Soften the butter in a bowl, work in the sugar with a wooden spoon and beat until light. Sift flour with salt and chocolate powder into a bowl, and stir into the mixture. Roll into balls the size of a small walnut, place well apart on a greased baking tray and flatten with a wet fork. Bake for 8-10 minutes, leave biscuits for 1-2 minutes on the tin before lifting on to a wire rack to cool.

To make the glacé icing : sift just over half the icing sugar into a basin and mix to a stiff paste with a little water, adding it 1 teaspoon at a time. Stand the basin in a saucepan of hot water and stir gently until the icing thins a little. Coat each biscuit with white icing and leave to set.

Mix the egg white with a fork, beat in sufficient sifted icing sugar to give a very stiff mixture; divide in two and colour one half pink and the other blue.

If you have the patience, pipe the initials of each child on the biscuits — pink for a girl, blue for a boy. You'll be surprised how quickly the biscuits disappear.

Quick ideas

Sandwiches. Cut them in fancy shapes, no more than $1\frac{1}{2}$ inches in length. Suggested fillings : creamed egg and cress ; cream cheese and chives ; tomatoes ; banana ; cherry jam.

Bridge rolls. Split in halves, butter and top each half with creamed egg, canned salmon and tomato — children like to see what they are expected to eat.

Cocktail sausages on sticks, bowls of **crisps** and **savoury biscuits** will disappear in a flash. These are best kept almost as a savoury course at the end, otherwise you may find sandwiches, biscuits and cakes remain untouched.

Small cakes. Bake in tiny petits fours cases — a basic Victoria sandwich mixture is the best and then variety can be introduced with coloured icing. Decorate the cakes with familiar sweets such as chocolate buttons, Smarties, etc. Shy children often refuse strange food at parties but if they recognise sweets they are well away.

The birthday cake should have on it the child's name, age and candles. Make a light sponge with soft icing (preferably without a butter cream filling which could be too rich for some children). Small boys go for cakes in the shape of the craze of the moment — engines, boats, or space ships.

Small meringues (unfilled) go down well placed on top of canned **fruit salad** (with fresh fruit added to it) or served separately. Make meringues as for field of mushrooms, left.

Maypole birthday cake

6 oz butter
grated rind and juice of
  1 medium-size orange
6 oz caster sugar
3 eggs (separated)
6 oz self-raising flour
pinch of salt

To make apricot glaze
5 tablespoons apricot jam
1-2 tablespoons water

For glacé icing
1 lb icing sugar
sugar syrup (made with 3 rounded
  tablespoons granulated sugar and
  $\frac{1}{4}$ pint water), or water (to mix)
few drops pink colouring
For royal icing (to decorate)
1 egg white
5-6 oz icing sugar (sifted)
mauve and yellow colourings

8-9 inch diameter sandwich tin
One $\frac{1}{2}$-inch dowel rod (6 or 12
* inches long)*
1 yard each narrow ribbon in four
* colours*
Few artificial flowers wired together
* in shape of a wreath*

Method

Grease and flour sandwich tin, set oven at 375°F or Mark 5.

Soften the butter with grated rind of the orange in a bowl; add sugar and beat until light and fluffy. Add the egg yolks one at a time and beat again. Sift flour and salt into a bowl; whisk egg whites until stiff. Fold in flour and strained juice of half the orange into the mixture, then fold in the egg whites. Turn at once into the prepared tin and bake in pre-set oven for about 40-45 minutes. Cool on a wire rack.

To make apricot glaze: put apricot jam and water into a pan, warm gently to dissolve jam, pour through a wire strainer, return to pan and boil gently until clear. Brush cake with hot apricot glaze and leave to set.

Watchpoint This coating of glaze is to prevent cake crumbs spoiling the appearance of the icing when this is poured and spread over the cake.

To make the glacé icing: sift the icing sugar, mix with strained juice of the second half of the orange and enough sugar syrup or water to make a really thick consistency. Add a few drops of colouring to make icing a pale shade of pink. Warm this icing gently. If done in a saucepan, take care that the mixture does not get too hot. At all times you must be able to hold the palm of your hand on base of the pan. The bain-marie method (see page 9) is safer for the amateur because icing loses its gloss if it gets too hot.

Spread icing over the cake.

To make the royal icing for decoration: lightly whisk the egg white; beat in the sifted icing sugar, 1 tablespoon at a time, and continue beating until the icing stands in peaks. Colour it in two or three pastel shades and shape or pipe small flowers around the top and bottom edge of the cake. Pipe child's name and age on top.

To make the maypole: twist the ribbons round and up the rod and secure with a dab of glue or adhesive tape, letting the ends fall from the wreath of flowers which is fixed firmly to the top. Place the maypole in the centre of the cake and let the ribbons fall on to the table and lead to a name card.

Numeral birthday cake

This makes an original birthday cake and frames in the shape of numerals 1 to 9 (and 0) can be bought at many large stores.

Method

Bake your Victoria sandwich mixture, as given in the maypole cake recipe, in the correct numeral frame for the child's age. When cool place cake on a board ready for icing; brush well with hot apricot glaze and leave until cold. Cover with glacé icing, decorate with child's name and candles.

A numeral 7 shape is easy to prepare without a special frame. Bake a Victoria sandwich mixture in the usual way in an 8-inch square tin. When cold, cut cake in two strips, 8 inches by 4 inches, and trim the ends. Fit together in the shape of a 7. Glaze, ice, decorate.

Home-made lemon drink

3 **lemons (unpeeled and diced)**
3 **tablespoons sugar**
1 **quart boiling water**
sprig of mint (optional)
ice
1-2 **extra slices of lemon**

Method

Wipe lemons and cut into dice — try not to lose any of the juice. Put into a jug (not a glass one) with the sugar. Pour on the boiling water, leave for 15-30 minutes until strong but without the taste becoming bitter; then strain. Put the mint into the serving jug with the ice and slices of fresh lemon 1 hour before the lemonade is wanted.

To make orange drink : simply squeeze juice from fresh oranges and add sugar to taste.

Weddings

We have suggestions for 3 kinds of wedding reception : a Buffet
lunch for 24 people, two menus for sit down lunches for the
same number, and some ideas for tea. Make our beautiful
wedding cake and remember to make it at least 2 months
ahead of the great day.

When catering for any large party it is essential to have most of
the preparation done beforehand and for this reason we have
chosen dishes which can be cooked in advance leaving only
garnishing, decoration and salads to be done on the day.

Wedding cake

Rich fruit cake

3 lb sultanas
3 lb currants
1 lb seedless raisins
1 lb muscatel raisins (seeded)
8 oz glacé cherries (halved)
4 oz almonds (blanched and
   shredded)
8 oz candied peel (finely shredded)
10 fl oz brandy
2½ lb plain flour
1 teaspoon salt
1 teaspoon ground cinnamon
1 nutmeg (grated)
1 tablespoon cocoa
2 lb butter
grated rind of 1 lemon and 1 orange
2 lb caster sugar
1 tablespoon black treacle
18 eggs
4 oz ground almonds

Cake tins (for sizes see page 97)

This amount will make a two-tiered cake using 12-inch and 8-inch round tins. If adapting this recipe for square cake tins, remember that they hold rather more mixture than the round ones, and a tiered cake (made with square tins) looks better if the tiers are not too deep.

Method
Prepare the cake tins, lining them with 4-5 thicknesses of greaseproof paper and tying a stout band of brown paper, or several thicknesses of newspaper, round the outside of the large tins so that the paper stands up about 2 inches round the rim. Don't grease inside paper at all as the cake mixture is very rich and will not stick.

Clean and prepare the fruit; place all in a large basin and sprinkle with half the brandy, cover and leave for 24 hours. Stir several times during this period so that the fruit soaks up all the liquid.

Sift the flour with the salt, spices and cocoa and then mix one-third of it with the prepared fruit. Cream the butter until soft, add the grated orange and lemon rind, and the sugar, and beat thoroughly until light and fluffy. It is best to beat with your hand for this quantity if an electric mixer is not available. Stir in the black treacle and beat in the eggs one at a time. Fold in the ground almonds and half the remaining flour, add the fruit and brandy mixture and lastly the rest of the flour. Turn into the prepared tins ready for baking, smooth the top with a palette knife and brush over with a little water. This helps to keep the cake soft on top in spite of the long baking.

For baking the cake the oven should be pre-set at 325°F or Mark 3. See the chart, page 97, for baking times. To keep cakes moist during baking, set large tins on several thicknesses of newspaper, and small tins inside a larger empty tin. This prevents the cakes from drying out.

Cover the cakes with a double thickness of brown paper when they are nicely coloured and reduce the heat to 300°F or Mark 2 after 3 hours.

It is quite possible to bake a two-tiered cake in a domestic oven, placing the smaller tin on a shelf above the large ▶

Wedding cake continued

bottom tier, but if three cakes are being made it is better to bake the bottom tier first and then the two smaller cakes. The uncooked mixture will not spoil if left in the tins overnight in a cool larder or refrigerator.

After baking, leave the cakes to cool in their tins for 30 minutes, and then carefully turn them on to wire racks, but leave the greaseproof paper on. When quite cold, wrap them in several more thicknesses of greaseproof paper and store in an airtight tin. The cakes are best if they are made three months before the wedding day.

During this time, say about every 4-5 weeks, unwrap the cakes, pierce them with a fine knitting needle and baste with about 5 tablespoons brandy. Rewrap and store as before. It is only necessary to pierce the cakes at the first soaking.

It is a good idea to bake an extra slab of cake for large weddings, when it is difficult to avoid a time lag between the bride cutting the cake and the guests eating it. Make this slab quite large and cover only the top with almond paste and icing. It can then be easily cut up 'behind the scenes' and added to the trays of cake being handed to the guests.

Almond paste

For about 2 lb quantity of marzipan
1 lb ground almonds
10 oz caster sugar
6 oz icing sugar (sifted)
1 large egg (or 2 small ones)
1 egg yolk
juice of $\frac{1}{2}$ lemon
1 tablespoon brandy, or rum, or sherry
$\frac{1}{2}$ teaspoon vanilla essence
2 tablespoons orange flower water

The quantity required will vary a little for each cake, depending on the depth of the cake in relation to the diameter, but for a good wedding cake you will need about half the weight of the cake in marzipan. (For a guide to amounts, see chart on page 97.)

Method
Place dry ingredients in a bowl and mix together; whisk the eggs and extra yolk with remaining ingredients, add this to the mixture of almonds and sugar, pounding lightly to release a little of the almond oil. Knead this mixture with the hand until smooth.

The almond paste should be put on about one week before the icing and decoration. This gives time for the paste to set and consequently the oil from the ground almonds is less likely to seep through the icing. A wedding cake should always have at least two coats of royal icing before it is decorated, to be sure of a good white colour.

Cover 6-8 $\frac{1}{2}$ inch diameter cake with the paste in the following way: brush or spread the cake thinly with hot apricot glaze, which prevents cake crumbs getting into the icing and also makes sure that the almond paste will stick to the cake. Now place almond paste on top of the cake, roll it so that it covers the top and falls down the side. Dust your hands with icing sugar and smooth paste firmly and evenly on to the side of the cake. Turn it upside down, press to flatten the paste on top and roll a bottle around the side to give a clean sharp edge.

For a larger cake it is wiser to use the following method: brush only the top of the cake with the hot apricot glaze. Roll out about half the marzipan to around the size of the cake top, using caster sugar to prevent it sticking to the slab or pastry board. Lift the cake, place it upside down on the paste and then, keeping your left hand firmly on the cake and rotating it gently, cut and mould the marzipan flush to the edge. Lift the cake over and brush away any crumbs. Take the remaining marzipan, knead it into a smooth long roll and press with the rolling pin to the depth of the cake.

Trim the edges and brush the paste with the hot glaze. Roll this strip round the cake (glazed side next to the cake) making a neat join and finish it by rolling it firmly with a straight-sided bottle or jam jar.

Royal icing

1 lb icing sugar
2 egg whites
1 teaspoon lemon juice, or orange flower water
$\frac{1}{2}$ teaspoon glycerine

Method

Pass the icing sugar through a fine nylon or hair sieve; whisk egg whites to a froth, add icing sugar, a tablespoonful at a time, beating thoroughly between each addition. Stir in flavouring and glycerine, continue beating until icing will stand in peaks.

Keep bowl covered with a damp cloth when using icing.

This icing sets very hard and is, therefore, particularly suitable for a tiered cake or for one that is to be stored for any length of time. Give the cake at least two flat coatings of royal icing before starting the decoration. The first coat need only be quite thin and should be left in a warm airy room to dry. The next day coat again with icing and allow it to dry in the same way before decorating as it is difficult to pipe on to a wet surface.

A very approximate guide to the quantity of icing needed is given in the chart (see page 97). The amount of icing needed, however, depends on the number and thickness of coatings and amount of decoration.

Cake boards

Choose the 'drum' type of board, ie. one that is $\frac{1}{2}$ inch thick; for bottom tier it should be 2 inches larger than cake, measured after coating twice.

For the smaller cakes the ▶

Wedding cake continued

board should be only 1 inch larger so that the decorative edging is piped close to the rim of the board. However, if the cake is to be mounted without pillars, place the second and third tiers on thin boards exactly the same size as the cakes.

Pillars, cake boards and other cake decorating equipment can be obtained by mail order from Hartley Smith (School of Cake Decorating), 34 Hampstead Road, London NW1.

Finishing
Store each tier in a separate box away from dust. On the wedding day mount them on a silver stand, place a small spray of flowers on the top to match the bride's bouquet.

Albumen-based powder can replace egg whites, lemon juice or glycerine in royal icing. Packed in 1, 2 or 4 oz quantities, it is obtainable from Hartley Smith. To use powder: whisk with a fork in water with chill taken off until dissolved; beat in icing sugar. 1 oz albumen powder is dissolved in $\frac{1}{2}$ pint water, which takes about $3\frac{1}{2}$ lb icing sugar.

Piping flowers

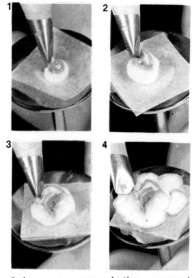

Colour one cup of the reserved icing bright pink. Fit a No. 58 petal pipe to a forcing bag. Spread a little of the bright pink icing down side of bag to thin end of pipe opening; lay knife blade over this, fill up with white icing and remove knife. Turn bag over so that thick end of pipe is pointing downwards.
1 *Attach 1-inch square of waxed paper to the flower spinner with icing. Turn it to form the flower centre*
2 *Pipe two more petals on to the centre piece still with the thick end of the pipe down. This will form a bud*
3 *Add a further three petals to the bud to make a medium-size flower. Make plenty of buds and flowers*
4 *For larger flowers: pipe five petals on to medium ones. Leave flowers 24 hours to dry, then remove paper*

	For 1-tier cake: Round 11-inch tin	For 1-tier cake: Square 12-inch tin	For 2-tier cake: Round or square 12-inch tin 8-inch tin	For 3-tier cake: Round or square 12-inch tin 8½-inch tin 6-inch tin
Rich fruit cake ingredients	$\frac{1}{2}$ quantity given	$\frac{3}{4}$ quantity given	quantity given	$1\frac{1}{4}$ quantity given
Baking time	$4\frac{1}{2}$ hours	5 hours	For 12-inch cake : 5 hours For 8-inch cake : 3 hours	For 12-inch cake : 5 hours For 8½-inch cake : 3½ hours For 6-inch cake : 2½ hours
For almond paste	5 lb marzipan	5-6 lb marzipan	For 12 inch cake : 5-6 lb marzipan For 8-inch cake : 2 lb marzipan	For 12-inch cake : 5-6 lb marzipan For 8½-inch cake : 2 lb marzipan For 6-inch cake : 1 lb marzipan
For royal icing	4-6 lb icing sugar	4-6 lb icing sugar	For 12-inch cake : 4-6 lb icing sugar For 8-inch cake : 2½-4 lb icing sugar	For 12-inch cake : 4-6 lb icing sugar For 8½-inch cake : 2½-4 lb icing sugar For 6-inch cake : 1½-2 lb icing sugar

Wedding cake continued

Icing and decorating

Place cake on a turntable. Spread the surplus icing down sides, adding more as required. Use plastic spatula at an angle of 45° and pull cake round until icing is smooth. Cover the board in same way

Place a No. 2 writing pipe in forcing bag. Fill it with white icing and pipe diagonal lines round the top edge of cake at $\frac{1}{4}$ - inch intervals, then repeat the lines in the opposite directions to form a lattice

Make the third and fourth lines of the lattice over the original ones, but make them slightly longer than the previous ones for a neat finish. Allow each layer of icing to dry before applying the next

Using a No. 42 shell pipe, make small shell shapes round the inner and outer edges of the lattice to cover up all the ends. Repeat the whole lattice process round the base of the cake and on the smaller tier

With a No. 2 writing pipe, mark rim of 3-inch diameter cup or tumbler with small icing drops. Then press drops ligthly on to top of lower tier at equal intervals to outline five circles

Using a No. 2 writing pipe in a bag filled with white icing, pipe on to side of the lower tier two loops between each circle, making ten loops altogether. Then pipe four similar loops on to upper tier side

Attach the flowers to the cake using icing from the No. 2 writing pipe. Taking the dots on top of the cake and the loops on the side as guiding lines, arrange the flowers in sizes as shown in the photograph

Thicken a little white icing with sifted icing sugar. Fill a plain forcing bag. Cut the bag so that there is a small slanting point. Pipe leaves between flowers on both cakes by holding the bag at an angle to the surface. Press with the thumb and then lift forcing bag away with a slight pull

Buffet lunch for 24

Salmon steaks en chaudfroid
Country style pâté
Turkey and tongue in aspic
Salade niçoise
Orange mousse with lychees
Strawberry gâteau

Sit-down meal 1 for 24

Consommé en gelée,
Beef en croûte
Stuffed spring chickens in
  aspic
Timbale aux fruits

Sit-down meal 2 for 24

Florida cocktail
Rice pilaf
Chicken Khoreshe
Charlotte mexicaine

Tea

make suitable quantities for 24

Sandwiches and rolls
Almond macaroons
Gâteau moka aux amandes
Coffee sponge fingers
Vanilla fork biscuits
Strawberry tartlets

Buffet lunch left to right : turkey and tongue in aspic ; cranberry sauce ; green salad ; strawberry gâteau ; salmon steaks en chaudfroid with salpicon of prawns, tomatoes and chopped aspic ; orange mousse with lychees ; salade niçoise ; salmon steaks

Salmon steaks en chaudfroid

12 salmon steaks (about 8 oz each)
2 pints court bouillon
1 tablespoon olive oil
1 shallot (finely chopped)
1 dessertspoon paprika pepper
1 dessertspoon tomato purée
juice strained from seeds of the tomato garnish
1½ pints mayonnaise
¾ oz gelatine
¾ pint aspic jelly

To garnish

1½ pints aspic jelly
fews sprigs of chervil, or strips of cucumber skin
12 tomatoes (skinned, seeds removed, and chopped)
½ lb shelled prawns, or shrimps

These can be made the evening before and kept in the refrigerator.

Method

Set oven at 350°F or Mark 4.

Cover the fish with hot court bouillon and poach the fish steaks in pre-set oven for about 20 minutes. Allow to cool a little in the liquid, then remove the skin and bones. Divide each steak in two and bind in muslin, then press between two plates until cold.

Meanwhile heat the oil, add the shallot and cook for a few minutes to soften it. Then add the paprika, tomato purée and strained juice from the tomato seeds and cook for 2-3 minutes; strain and cool. Place the fish steaks on a cake rack with a tray underneath.

Flavour the mayonnaise with tomato and paprika mixture; dissolve the gelatine in the $\frac{3}{4}$ pint of aspic over gentle heat and add to the mayonnaise. When on the point of setting, baste over the salmon steaks.

Decorate each steak with the chervil or strips of cucumber skin (dipped in aspic) and then baste again with cool aspic. Arrange on a serving platter and garnish with a salpicon of the tomatoes, prawns and remaining aspic jelly (chopped).

(A photograph of the finished salmon steaks is shown on pages 100 - 101.)

After being poached the salmon steaks are divided in two and the skin and bones are removed

Coating salmon steaks with the flavoured mayonnaise and aspic mixture on the point of setting

Country style pâté (Pâté de campagne)

3 Ostend (tame) rabbits
1 clove of garlic (crushed with
  ½ teaspoon salt)
3 tablespoons chopped parsley
3 wineglasses white wine
1 glass brandy (2 fl oz)
pinch of ground mace
3 lb gammon (uncooked)
1 calf's foot, or knuckle of veal
bouquet garni
salt and pepper
2 oz luting paste
melted lard (to cover)

2-3 terrines

Pâté can be made up to 7 days in advance and stored in the refrigerator.

Luting paste is a flour and water mixture of a consistency similar to that of scone dough. To seal a casserole or terrine, put 3-4 oz flour into a bowl and mix quickly with cold water to a firm dough 4 oz flour will take ⅛ pint water).

Method

Cut good 'fillets' from thighs and back of rabbit; chop the remaining meat with the rabbit livers, crushed clove of garlic and chopped parsley and marinate for 1 hour in two-thirds of the white wine, the brandy and mace.

Put the gammon and calf's foot (or veal knuckle) in a pan with water to cover, remaining glass of white wine, bouquet garni and seasoning and simmer gently. After 40 minutes remove the gammon but continue cooking calf's foot to make a good jelly. Chop gammon roughly and mix with the marinated mixture.

Fill 2-3 terrines with alternate layers of farce and fillets, starting and finishing with the farce, seasoning each layer of fillets carefully. Cover with a lid and seal with luting paste; cook au bain-marie at 350-375°F or Mark 4-5 for 2 hours.

When pâté is cooked, remove luting paste and press lightly for 12 hours; pour over a protective layer of melted lard. Store in refrigerator until needed. The day before serving, scrape off the layer of lard, turn out the pâté and baste with jellied stock. Alternatively, the pâté can be served in the pot with the layer of lard.

Turkey and tongue in aspic

1 turkey (10-12 lb)
3-3½ lb smoked tongue
sliced onion, carrot, celery (to flavour)
large bouquet garni
1½ oz butter
1½ oz flour
1 pint milk
salt and white pepper
½ lb gammon (cooked)
1 teaspoon Dijon mustard
¾ pint mayonnaise
2 pints aspic jelly
watercress (to garnish)
cranberry sauce (canned) — for serving

This can be made 1-2 days beforehand and kept in a cool larder or in refrigerator.

Method
Roast the turkey following your favourite method, eg. French roasting — 15 minutes per lb and 15 minutes over at 350°F or Mark 4; or slow roasting — 20 minutes per lb, 30 minutes over, at 325° or Mark 3.

Simmer the tongue in water to cover, with flavouring vegetables and herbs, for 3-3½ hours and leave to cool in the liquid.

Prepare a white sauce in the usual way with the butter, flour and milk and season lightly. Cover with a buttered paper to prevent skin forming and cool.

Remove the skin and trim the root of the tongue, taking away any small bones, and pass the meat through a mincer. Mince the gammon and pound it with the tongue and cold sauce; work in the French mustard and mayonnaise. Cover to exclude air and so preserve the pink colour, and keep this 'mousse' in refrigerator until ready to dish up.

To shred the turkey: take off legs and thighs of the bird, remove meat from the bones in the largest possible pieces and then cut into long neat shreds. Remove all the dark meat from the carcass and cut in the same way; put all this meat in a deep tray, then shred the white meat and lay carefully on top. Spoon the tongue mousse on to 2 large shallow oval dishes and smooth with a palette knife. Lift the shredded turkey very carefully with a fish slice and place over the top.

Put the aspic into a thin saucepan and stand it in cold water with a few ice cubes; stir aspic very gently until on the point of setting, then spoon it quickly over the turkey.

Garnish with watercress just before putting on the table. Serve with cranberry sauce and a selection of salads.

Salade niçoise

2 lb tomatoes
2 lb French beans
1 cucumber (peeled and shredded)
¼ lb black olives (stoned)
¼ pint French dressing (see page 40)

This salad is particularly good with the country-style pâte and the turkey and tongue in aspic.

Method
Scald, skin and quarter tomatoes. Cut beans into large diamonds and boil until tender; drain and refresh. Mix all the ingredients together and moisten with French dressing.

Orange mousse with lychees

3 eggs
2 egg yolks
3 oz caster sugar
$\frac{1}{2}$ oz gelatine
5 tablespoons water
$\frac{1}{4}$ pint double cream
1 can frozen orange juice

To finish

1 large can lychees
$\frac{1}{4}$ pint double cream
angelica, or pistachio nuts

Angel cake tin (lightly oiled)

Serves 8 people

Method
Place the whole eggs and yolks in a basin, add the sugar and whisk over a pan of hot water until thick. Remove from the heat and continue whisking until cold. If using an electric beater no heat is necessary, but the mixture must be so thick that when lifted on the beaters it will fall and leave a trail.

Soak gelatine in the water and dissolve it over heat. Partially whip the first $\frac{1}{4}$ pint of cream and quickly stir this, the orange juice and gelatine into the egg mousse; as mixture begins to set, pour it into tin.

Cover mousse with foil and leave to set in the refrigerator tor two hours or longer. Turn it out on serving dish and fill centre with the drained lychees. Decorate with rosettes of whipped cream and angelica or pistachio nuts.

Strawberry gâteau

3 oz plain flour
$\frac{1}{2}$ teaspoon ground cinnamon
pinch of salt
3 eggs
$3\frac{3}{4}$ oz caster sugar
grated rind of $\frac{1}{2}$ lemon

To finish

1 lb strawberries
$\frac{1}{2}$ pint double cream
2-3 drops of vanilla essence
1 tablespoon caster sugar
extra cream (to decorate)

8-9 inch diameter cake tin

Serves 8 people

Method
Set oven at 350°F or Mark 4 and grease tin. Sift flour with the cinnamon and a good pinch of salt and set aside.

Break eggs into a bowl, add the sugar gradually and whisk over pan of hot water until thick and mousse-like; then remove from heat and continue whisking until the mixture is cold. Fold in sifted flour and grated lemon rind; turn mixture into tin and bake for 15-20 minutes. Turn on to rack to cool.

Whip cream, add essence, sugar and a quarter of the strawberries, sliced. Split cake, sandwich with this mixture and slide on to serving plate. Arrange rest of strawberries (whole) on top and decorate with rosettes of cream.

Consommé en gelée

10 cans (12-15 oz) consommé
¼ pint sherry — optional
2 tablespoons tomato purée — optional
pepper (ground from mill)

For serving
1 wedge of lemon per portion
1 teaspoon red caviar per portion (optional)

This recipe uses canned consommé to save time.

Method

Keep cans in a warm room before opening, then turn out into a large jug and add sherry, if wished (1 tablespoon of sherry to every 2 cans). If adding to tomato purée mix it with a little of the soup before adding it to the main bulk. Grind in a little pepper from the mill and put consommé in the refrigerator overnight.

Serve in soup cups and place a wedge of lemon in each saucer. For something special, stir a small spoonful of red caviar into each soup cup before serving — only do this if the soup is served cold. (The consommé can, of course, be served hot if preferred.)

> Consommé en gelée can be made the day before it is needed and stored in a cool larder.

Beef en croûte

2 lb fillet of beef
8 oz quantity of puff pastry (see page 10)
pepper
butter (to sauté and roast)
4 oz button mushrooms
1 dessertspoon chopped mixed herbs and parsley
egg (for glazing)
watercress, or parsley (to garnish)

These quantities serve 4-6 people. Quantities for 24 guests are given right. If it is to be served cold it can be made the day before. If hot, do the preliminary cooking the day before, wrap meat in the pastry and keep in refrigerator. Bake it on the day.

Method

First prepare the pastry and keep well chilled in the refrigerator overnight. Set oven at 425°F or Mark 7.

Trim and tie up the fillet; pepper it and brown it quickly all over in hot butter, then roast in oven for 10 minutes. Take out and allow to get cold; remove string or thread. In the meantime slice mushrooms and sauté them in butter for a few minutes; draw pan aside, add the herbs, and cool.

Roll out the puff pastry to a rectangle. Divide it in two, one piece two-thirds larger than the other. Put the mushroom mixture on the larger piece, lay the beef on top and press up the pastry round it. Lay the other piece of pastry over the top, pressing the edges together well, brush with egg glaze and decorate with 'fleurons' of pastry. Bake in pre-set oven for 35-40 minutes or until well browned.

Serve beef hot or cold, garnished with watercress or parsley. If hot, serve a demi-glace, or madère, sauce separately and vegetables of choice. If cold, serve with a selection of salads.

Quantities for 24 people

3 fillets of beef (each 2½-3 lb)
3 pieces of puff pastry (each 12 oz)
pepper
approximately 6-8 oz butter
1 lb button mushrooms
2 rounded tablespoons chopped
mixed herbs and parsley
1 beaten egg (for glazing)
watercress, or parsley

Stuffed spring chickens in aspic

(Poussins farcis en gelée)

14 double poussins
1¾ lb veal, or pork (minced)
1 medium-size onion (finely chopped)
2 oz butter
1 rounded tablespoon chopped thyme and parsley
1 pint measure (6 oz) of fresh breadcrumbs
2 small eggs (beaten)
salt and pepper

To roast
½-¾ lb butter
2 pints strong stock (made from the giblets)

To garnish
aspic jelly
watercress

These can be made the day before and garnished on the day. Store in the refrigerator.

Method

Ask your butcher to partially bone out the poussins; season the cut surface. Soften the onion in the butter, cool, then add it to the minced veal (or pork) with the herbs and crumbs. Mix well, bind with the egg and season well. Divide this farce equally between the poussins, reshape them, sew up and truss. Spread butter thickly on grease-proof paper or foil, tuck this over and round the poussins, and pour enough stock into the roasting tin just to cover the bottom. Roast at 400°F or Mark 6 for 35-40 minutes, basting well and turning the birds over 2 or 3 times; add more stock to the tin if necessary.

Take up birds, deglaze the tin with stock and pour off into a bowl. Leave to get quite cold. When the poussins are cold also, remove strings, split and trim. Arrange poussins down long serving dishes.

Scoop off the butter from the gravy and spoon the jelly over the chicken. Garnish dish with watercress and 'croutes' of aspic jelly. Serve with appropriate salads, eg. potato mayonnaise or vinaigrette, or rice salad; cucumber and melon vinaigrette; tomato salad.

Timbale aux fruits (Sponge cake with fruit)

2 eggs
4 oz caster sugar
2-3 drops of vanilla essence
3 oz flour
fresh fruit salad (made with about
$\frac{1}{4}$ pint heavy syrup flavoured
with vanilla, rum or kirsch)
apricot jam
shredded almonds

*Ring mould (1 $\frac{1}{2}$ pints capacity)
plain or fluted*

Choose fresh fruit in season:
eg. 6 oz strawberries, 2 ripe
pears, 6 oz black grapes and
2 bananas.

This size cake serves 6 people.
The sponge can be made the
day before and stored in an airtight tin; finish off on the day.

Method

Set oven at 350°F or Mark 4.
Butter mould and dust first with
sugar and then with flour.

Whisk the eggs and sugar
together in a bowl over hot
water; when really thick and
mousse-like remove from the
heat and whisk for a few
minutes more.

Add vanilla essence to mixture, sift in the flour, cutting and
folding it in with a metal spoon.
Turn at once into prepared ring
mould. Bake in pre-set oven for
25-30 minutes or until firm to
the touch. Turn out and cool.

Spoon a little of the syrup
from the fruit salad over the
cake to moisten and flavour it;
arrange some fruit in the centre.
Boil a little of the syrup with
1-2 tablespoons apricot jam to
make a light glaze, spoon this
over the cake and scatter over
the almonds. Arrange rest of
fruit round the edge.

For 24 people

Make two cakes baked in
large ring moulds 2-2 $\frac{1}{2}$ pints
capacity). For each cake double
the above quantities of ingredients and bake for 45-50
minutes. Double also the
quantity of fruit and syrup for
each cake.

*For heavy syrup use 3 oz sugar to
$\frac{1}{4}$ pint liquid*

Florida cocktail

12 oranges
10 grapefruit
caster sugar, or sugar syrup

Coupe glasses

Choose especially fine grapefruit and oranges — thin-skinned
and heavy.

Method
Slice the peel and pith from the
fruit, cutting out the sections
from between the membranes;
dust lightly with sugar, or
moisten with sugar syrup. Chill
cocktail a little, then spoon into
the glasses just before serving.

Rice pilaf

1 onion (chopped)
$2\frac{1}{2}$ oz butter
8 oz rice
$1\frac{1}{4}$ pints chicken stock
3 oz seeded raisins
2 oz almonds (shredded and
   toasted)

This quantity serves 5-6 people.

Method
Set oven at 350°F or Mark 4.
Soften onion in half the butter
in a flameproof casserole, add
rice and after 1-2 minutes add
stock and raisins. Bring to the
boil, cover and cook in pre-set
oven for about 20 minutes or
until the rice is tender and the
stock absorbed.

Fork in the almonds, dot the
surface of the rice with the
rest of the butter, cover the pan
and leave in the oven for 5
minutes before serving.

Quantities for 24 people

3 onions
6 oz butter
$2\frac{1}{4}$ lb rice
5-$5\frac{1}{2}$ pints chicken stock
1 lb seeded raisins
8 oz almonds

Chicken Khoreshe

2 chickens (each 2 lb), or one 3 lb
  chicken
butter (to sauté)
2-3 large aubergines
2 large onions (sliced)
1 green pepper (shredded and
  blanched)
1 lb tomatoes (skinned, seeds
  removed, and sliced)
salt and pepper
grated rind of $\frac{1}{2}$, and the juice of
  1, large lemon
oil (to sauté)
good pinch of saffron (soaked
  in 3 tablespoons water)

This quantity serves 5-6 people.

The first stage of cooking
(before the aubergine slices
are added) can be done the
day before. On the day, the
aubergines should be prepared
and added and dish should be
cooked in oven at 350°F or
Mark 4 for 30-35 minutes.

Method
Slice aubergines $\frac{1}{4}$ inch thick,
sprinkle with salt and place
them in a colander to drain,
weighted down with a plate.

Set oven at 350°F or Mark 4.
Cut the chickens into neat
joints and brown in butter,
arrange them in a casserole or
deep baking dish in layers with
the onions, pepper and tomatoes; season, add lemon juice
and rind. Cover tightly and cook
in pre-set oven for about 1 hour.

Meanwhile dry the aubergine
slices and brown quickly in oil.
Pour the saffron liquid over the
ingredients in the casserole,
adding a little jellied stock if
necessary, and place the aubergine slices on top. Return the
dish to the oven, uncovered,
and cook for a further 15
minutes. Serve hot with new
potatoes and French beans or
with a rice pilaf.

Note : the onions may be
blanched after slicing.

Quantities for 24 people

5 chickens (each $3\frac{1}{2}$ lb)
6-8 oz butter
10 large aubergines
10 large onions
5-6 green peppers
5 lb tomatoes
5 large lemons
$\frac{1}{2}$ pint oil
1 dessertspoon saffron (soaked
  in a teacup of water)

Charlotte mexicaine

1 lb dessert chocolate
1½ pints strong coffee (freshly made)
4 egg yolks
4 oz granulated sugar
1 oz gelatine (dissolved in ¼ pint water)
¾ pint double cream
2-3 egg whites (stiffly whipped)

To decorate
langues de chats biscuits
¼ - ½ pint double cream
chocolate dragées

8-inch diameter cake tin

This size charlotte serves 12 people. It can be made the day before and decorated on the day; keep it in the refrigerator.

Method

Lightly oil cake tin.

Cream egg yolks thoroughly with the sugar.

Break up the chocolate, put it in a saucepan with a little of the coffee and melt it over a gentle heat. When smooth, add the rest of the coffee and bring to the boil, stirring continually. Pour the boiling chocolate and coffee mixture on to the yolks and sugar, blend and allow to cool. Add gelatine solution to the mixture; when on the point of setting, fold in cream and lastly the whipped egg whites. Turn mixture into prepared cake tin to set.

When set, turn charlotte on to a serving plate, spread the sides with a little extra whipped cream and press the biscuits round the edges, overlapping each one. Decorate with rosettes of cream and the dragées.

For 24 people

Allow double the quantity of this recipe to make two charlottes.

Sandwiches and rolls

Asparagus rolls. Cut crust off a small brown loaf; butter and cut into thin slices. Place a cooked asparagus head on each slice and roll up.

Smoked salmon roulades. Cut crust off bottom of small brown loaf; butter and cut in thin slices lengthways. Cover each slice with smoked salmon, sprinkle with lemon juice and black pepper. Trim away remaining crust and roll each slice like a swiss roll. Wrap in greaseproof paper and chill (overnight if wished) and slice thinly before serving.

Ribbon sandwiches. Cut a small brown loaf as for salmon roulades, but butter both sides of middle slices. Make four different coloured fillings, eg. pink — chopped cooked ham, crisp bacon and pimiento; yellow — hard-boiled egg yolks; white — cream cheese; green — finely chopped watercress mixed with pickle. Alternate fillings between slices; reshape into loaf, wrap in foil or damp cloth and chill for at least 3 hours. Cut into slices.

Almond macaroons

7 oz caster sugar
1 oz granulated sugar
4 oz ground almonds
$\frac{1}{2}$ oz rice flour
2-3 egg whites (according to size)
2-3 drops of vanilla essence
rice paper
split almonds

This makes approximately 9.

Method
Set oven at 350°F or Mark 4.

Mix the sugars, ground almonds and rice flour together in a mixing bowl; add the egg whites and the essence and beat all together with a wooden spoon for about 5 minutes. Scrape down sides of bowl; allow to stand for 5 minutes.

Meanwhile cut the rice paper into 3-inch squares and place, shiny side down, on a dry baking sheet. Continue beating the almond mixture for 5 minutes more until thick and white. Using a bag and $\frac{1}{2}$-inch pipe, shape neatly on to rice paper squares, place a split almond in the centre of each macaroon and bake in pre-set oven for 20-30 minutes.

Gâteau moka aux amandes

3 oz plain flour
pinch of salt
3 eggs
4½ oz caster sugar

To finish
butter cream
coffee essence (to flavour)
3 oz almonds (blanched, split
  and shredded)
icing sugar

9½-inch diameter layer cake tin

This gives about 10 portions.
The cake can be made and
decorated the day before ; store
it in an airtight tin.

Method
Set the oven at 370°F or Mark
4-5. Prepare the tin.

Sift the flour with salt. Break
the eggs into a bowl, add the
sugar gradually and then whisk
over a pan of hot water until
the mixture is thick and white
(and forms a ribbon trail).
Remove bowl from the heat and
continue beating until the bowl
is cold. Fold the flour into the
mixture, using a tablespoon.
Pour the mixture at once into the
tin and bake it in pre-set oven
for 25-30 minutes. Turn the
cake on to a wire rack to cool.

Have ready the butter cream

well flavoured with the coffee essence. Bake almonds to a light golden-brown.

Split the cake and sandwich with a thin layer of the coffee butter cream. Reshape and spread the top and sides with more of the same cream, press the browned almonds all over the cake, dredge lightly with icing sugar and then decorate round the top edge with rosettes of butter cream.

Butter cream

2 oz granulated sugar
4 tablespoons water
2 egg yolks
6 oz unsalted butter

Method
Dissolve the sugar in the water in a saucepan over gentle heat, then boil it steadily until the syrup will form a 'thread' (216-218°F on a sugar thermometer). Pour the syrup on to the egg yolks and whisk until thick and mousse-like. Cream the butter until soft, add the egg mousse by degrees. Flavour and use.

Coffee sponge fingers

4 eggs
6 oz caster sugar
4 oz flour
almonds (blanched, shredded
    and browned) — to decorate
icing sugar (for dredging)

For butter icing
3 oz butter
6 oz icing sugar
coffee essence (to colour
    and flavour)

Tin, or paper case (9 inches by 5 inches)

This makes 15-18 fingers.

Method
Break the eggs, add the sugar gradually and then whisk in a bowl over a pan of hot water until thick and mousse-like. Remove from the heat and continue beating until the bowl is quite cold. Fold in the finely sifted flour and turn at once into a prepared paper case or tin and bake in pre-set oven at 350°F or Mark 4 for about 10 minutes.

Meanwhile make the butter icing: cream the butter, add the finely sifted icing sugar by degrees, beating well between each addition. Add the essence to taste.

When the sponge is cool, trim it and spread the top thickly and evenly with coffee butter icing. Press the shredded browned almonds over, dredge with icing sugar, and put in a cold place to set. Cut into fingers 1 inch wide.

Vanilla fork biscuits

4 oz butter
2 oz caster sugar
5 oz self-raising flour
2-3 drops of vanilla essence

These quantities make approximately 8-12 biscuits.

Method

Set oven at 375°F or Mark 5-6.
Soften the butter with a wooden spoon, add the sugar, and cream until white. Stir in the flour and vanilla essence. Roll the mixture into balls the size of a walnut, place on a greased baking sheet and flatten with a fork. Bake in pre-set oven for 7-8 minutes.

Redcurrant jelly glaze

Beat the redcurrant jelly with a fork or small whisk until it liquefies, then rub through a strainer into a small saucepan. Heat gently without stirring until quite clear (boiling will spoil both colour and flavour). When brushing this glaze over the fruit use a very soft brush. Always work from the centre outwards, drawing the brush, well laden with the glaze, towards the edge.

Strawberry tartlets

For rich shortcrust pastry
5 oz plain flour
pinch of salt
3 oz butter
1 teaspoon caster sugar
1 egg yolk
$1\frac{1}{2}$-2 tablespoons cold water

For filling
8 oz strawberries
redcurrant jelly glaze

Small tartlet tins

Method

Make the rich shortcrust pastry and set aside to chill. Line the pastry on to the small tartlet tins and bake blind (or about 8 minutes in an oven at 375°F or Mark 5). Allow to cool.
Hull (remove stalks from) the strawberries and keep on one side. Warm the redcurrant jelly glaze but do not boil. Brush the cases with the jelly, arrange strawberries in the cases and brush again with the glaze. The amount of glaze should be generous — sufficient to fill the pastry cases and so hold strawberries firmly in place.

21st Birthday Party

Our 21st Birthday Party is designed for 50 guests and it's a good idea when catering for such large numbers to offer a wide variety of dishes. Here are 2 starters : a prawn and egg mousse or sweetbread bouchées. For the main course serve a galantine of turkey and cold roast beef with a selection of salads. There are 3 sweets to offer. Pride of place should be given to the birthday cake.

Quantities for a party of 50 people

Bouchées toulousaines : the recipe here makes about 30 cases with filling.

Prawn and egg mousse : each mousse gives about 12 portions, so make three for 36 portions.

Galantine of turkey : using a 12-lb bird, the galantine should give about 25-30 portions. Use two birds for 50 portions.

Roast beef : a 10-lb joint of sirloin or wing rib will give plenty of servings for those who prefer plain meat.

Fruit salad : the recipe here gives 10 portions.

Salads
Each recipe gives about 20-30 servings, according to size of the portions.

For celery and French bean salad : allow 4 lb French beans, 6-8 heads of celery and $\frac{3}{4}$-1 pint French dressing.

For sweetcorn and pickled onion salad : allow 5 cans of sweetcorn kernels and 3 jars of silverskin onions. Use $\frac{1}{2}$ pint French dressing.

Gâteau Diane : the recipe here gives 10 portions. Make four gâteaux in advance and fill them the evening before the party.

For potato salad : use 7 lb potatoes to give 36 portions. You will need 1 pint French dressing to mix with potatoes while still warm, and 2 pints mayonnaise. Use 1 pint mayonnaise for mixing with potatoes and remainder for coating them in serving dish.

Gâteau mille feuilles au citron : the recipe here will make three gâteaux in all, each one giving 10 portions. The lemon curd filling and 1 lb apricot jam glaze will be enough for all three gâteaux mille feuilles.

Finished dishes for the 21st buffet party : (from left to right)
Bouchées toulousaines, galantine of turkey, cold roast beef, prawn and egg mousse, sweetcorn and pickled onion salad, beetroot and horseradish relish, celery and French bean salad, fruit salad, gâteau Diane, and gâteau mille feuilles au citron.

Bouchées toulousaines

(Sweetbread bouchées)

1 lb quantity of puff pastry (see
page 10)
egg wash (for brushing)

For filling
1½ lb lambs sweetbreads
6 oz button mushrooms (sliced)
½ oz butter
¾ pint béchamel sauce (made
with 3 oz butter, 3 oz flour and
¾ pint stock from the sweetbreads)
3-4 tablespoons creamy milk, or
cream
6 oz cooked, sliced ham
(shredded)

*2½-inch and 1½-inch diameter pastry
cutters*

Method

Set oven at 425°F or Mark 7.
Roll out the pastry just over
¼ inch thick, brush lightly with
egg wash, then stamp out into
rounds with the large cutter.
Make an incision in the centre
with the smaller cutter. Lift
rounds on to a dampened baking
sheet, then chill for a few
minutes before baking in pre-
set hot oven for 15-20 minutes
until bouchées are well risen
and russet-brown. (If eaten
cold, the pastry is more palatable
when well cooked.) Lift them
on to a rack to cool.

To prepare sweetbreads :
soak them for several hours in
salted water, with 1-2 slices of
lemon or a few drops of vinegar,
if wished. Then rinse them, put
in a pan of cold water with a
little salt and a slice of lemon
and bring them slowly to the
boil. Remove any scum as it
rises to the surface. Strain the
sweetbreads, reserving ¾ pint
of the liquid for the béchamel
sauce. Rinse them quickly and
remove any ducts or skin. Press
them lightly between two
plates, with a 2-lb weight on
top, and leave until cold. Then
cut them in small pieces.

To prepare filling : sauté the
mushrooms in ½ oz butter for
3-4 minutes. Make the béchamel
sauce (see page 9), finishing with
the creamy milk (or cream),
then draw pan aside. While
sauce is still hot, add mushrooms, ham and sweetbreads.
If mixture is too stiff, add a
little extra milk (or cream).

Split the bouchées and put
a good spoonful of the filling
into each one. Serve them
either hot or cold.

To reheat filled bouchées :
place them on a baking sheet or
ovenproof serving dish and put
in moderate oven at 350°F or
Mark 4 for 20 minutes.

Prawn and egg mousse

8 oz prawns (frozen, or fresh) —
  peeled and very finely chopped
12 eggs (hard-boiled and peeled)
¾ pint mayonnaise (see page 10)
2 egg whites
1½ oz gelatine
¼ pint stock, or wine, or water
salt and pepper

For béchamel sauce
2 oz butter
2 oz flour
1 pint milk (flavoured with 1 teaspoon paprika pepper and 1
  teaspoon tomato purée)

For devilled garnish
1 lb tomatoes
8 oz prawns (frozen, or fresh)
  — peeled
2-3 drops of Tabasco sauce
1 teaspoon tomato ketchup
3 tablespoons French dressing
small cress, or cucumber, or
  watercress and extra slices of
  tomato

Ring mould (2¼ pints capacity)

Method

First oil the mould, then divide
the hard-boiled eggs in half,
remove the yolks and rub them
through a wire strainer; chop
the egg whites.

Prepare the béchamel sauce
(see page 9) and, when cold,
pound with the prawns and
sieved egg yolks until smooth,
then work in the mayonnaise.

Stiffly whip the egg whites;
dissolve the gelatine in the
stock (or wine or water) and
add to the mayonnaise mixture
with the chopped egg whites
and season well. As the mixture
begins to thicken, fold in the
egg whites. Turn mousse into
the oiled mould and leave to
set (about 2 hours).

Prepare the garnish. Scald
and skin the tomatoes and cut
them into four. Remove the
hard core and the seeds, then
cut the flesh into fine shreds.
Add the Tabasco sauce and
tomato ketchup to the French
dressing and mix this with the
tomatoes and prawns.

When the mousse is set, turn
it out on a large dish and fill the
centre with the devilled tomatoes and prawns. Garnish the
dish with a salad of your choice:
small cress, cucumber, watercress and extra slices of tomato.

*Above: pounding béchamel with
prawns and sieved yolks*
*Below: garnishing prawn and egg
mousse with the watercress*

121

Galantine of turkey

12 lb turkey
3-4 tablespoons salad oil
2 glasses sherry
$\frac{1}{2}$ pint jellied stock

For stuffing

6 oz butter
2 onions (finely chopped)
2 lb cooked ham (shoulder cut)
— minced
1 lb raw veal (minced)
12 oz fresh white breadcrumbs
1 tablespoon mixed chopped
herbs
grated rind and juice of 2
oranges
salt and pepper
1 egg (beaten)

For serving

1 quart aspic jelly (see page 9)
bouquets of watercress

Trussing needle and fine string

Method

Ask the butcher to bone out your turkey.

To prepare stuffing: melt butter, add onion, cook until it is soft but not coloured and allow to cool. Mix ham, veal, breadcrumbs and herbs together. Add orange rind and juice, season and bind mixture with beaten egg.

Spread stuffing over turkey, roll it up and sew with fine string, then tie at intervals along galantine to keep stuffing in position. Set oven at 350°F or Mark 4.

Heat oil in a roasting tin, add galantine, pour over sherry and stock and baste well. Cover with a piece of buttered paper or foil and cook for 3-3$\frac{1}{2}$ hours in pre-set moderate oven, reducing heat to 325°F or Mark 3 for the last hour when galantine will be well coloured. Turn and baste it every 20 minutes throughout the cooking, adding extra stock, if necessary, to keep it moist. Remove galantine from tin and allow it to cool. Then wrap in foil and keep in refrigerator before finishing the next day.

To finish galantine: after removing string, brush it with cool aspic, on the point of setting. Cut meat in even slices and arrange these on a large serving dish; baste them with cool, but still liquid, aspic and allow to set. Garnish dish with watercress, and serve with a variety of salads.

Celery and French bean salad

4 lb French beans (fresh, or frozen)
6 heads of celery, or 8, if very small
$\frac{1}{4}$-1 pint French dressing (see page 40)

Method

If using fresh French beans, trim and cut them into lozenge-shapes before cooking; if using frozen beans, cook and cut them into lozenge-shapes after cooking. In both cases, cook beans until tender (about 10-15 minutes for fresh ones) in boiling, salted water, then drain and refresh them well, as this helps to preserve the colour.

Wash and trim the celery, cut into 1-inch pieces, then again into julienne strips. Leave these in ice-cold water until ready to use. Then drain and dry celery well, mix together with the French beans and add the French dressing. Turn into bowls for serving.

Beetroot and horseradish relish

6-8 large cooked beetroot (about 2 lb in all)
4 oz finely grated horseradish (fresh, or bottled variety, preserved in vinegar only and drained)
1 teaspoon dry mustard
$\frac{1}{2}$ teaspoon salt
$\frac{1}{2}$ teaspoon black pepper
1 tablespoon caster sugar
3 tablespoons red wine vinegar
$\frac{1}{2}$ pint sour cream, or $\frac{1}{2}$ pint double cream (soured with about $\frac{1}{2}$ teaspoon lemon juice)

Method

Grate the beetroot and mix with the horseradish. Mix all the seasonings and sugar with the wine vinegar and stir into the sour cream. Mix this with the beetroot and horseradish and turn into bowls for serving.

Gâteau Diane

4 **egg whites**
8 **oz caster sugar**

For filling
8 **oz plain block chocolate**
4 **fl oz water**
1 **pint double cream**

For decoration
2 **oz chocolate caraque (see right)**

The meringue rounds can be made at least one week before the party and stored in airtight tins. They should be packed in layers one on top of the other with a layer of greaseproof paper between each round.

the same cream and decorate with the chocolate caraque (see right). The cake must be filled at least 2-3 hours before serving and can be done the day before, providing it is left in the refrigerator overnight. This will keep the meringue soft enough to cut, but the covering of cream by excluding the air will prevent the meringue from becoming too soft.

A slice of the gâteau Diane, made with three meringue rounds spread with chocolate cream, and decorated with chocolate caraque

Method
Line 3 baking sheets with non-stick kitchen paper; set oven at 250-300°F or Mark$\frac{1}{2}$-1.

Prepare the meringue by beating the egg whites until stiff and adding half the sugar. Whisk mixture until stiff, then fold in the remaining sugar. Spread or pipe the mixture into 3 thin rounds, 8-9 inches in diameter, on the prepared baking sheets. Bake meringues in pre-set cool oven for about 50-60 minutes, or longer, until they are dry and crisp.

To make the filling: break the chocolate into small pieces, put it in a pan with the water and dissolve over very gentle heat. Tip chocolate into a bowl and allow to cool. Whip the cream until it begins to thicken, then add the chocolate and continue beating until it is thick.

To serve: spread each round with the chocolate cream and layer one on top of the other. Spread the top and sides with

Chocolate caraque

Grate 3 oz of plain chocolate or of chocolate couverture (cooking chocolate). Melt it on a plate over a pan of hot water and work with a palette knife until smooth. Spread this thinly on a marble slab or laminated surface and leave until nearly set. Then, using a long sharp knife, shave it off the slab slantwise, using a slight sawing movement and holding the knife almost upright. The chocolate will form long scrolls or flakes. These will keep in an airtight tin but look better when they are freshly made.

Shaving off long scrolls or flakes with a palette knife to make the chocolate caraque

Gâteau mille feuilles au citron

1¼ lb quantity of puff pastry
   (see page 10)
2¼ pints double cream
1 lb apricot glaze

For lemon curd filling
8 oz caster sugar
4 oz unsalted butter
grated rind and juice of 2 large
   lemons
3 eggs (well beaten)

For decoration
crystallised fruits
almonds, or pistachio nuts

4-5 inch diameter plain cutter

Above : decorating gâteau mille feuilles with small pastry shapes, crystallised fruit and rosettes of whipped cream

Method

Set oven at 400°F or Mark 6, and dampen a baking sheet.

Roll out pastry very thinly and cut 6 rounds the size of a dessert plate; remove the centres of each round with the cutter to leave a large ring of pastry. From remaining pastry cut 3 plain circles, a little thicker and larger than the rings, to form bases for each cake.

Place the pastry rings on the baking sheet, prick them well with a fork and bake in pre-set hot oven for 8 minutes. Then prick and bake the circles on a dampened baking sheet for 12-15 minutes. Make any pastry trimmings into tiny stars, diamonds, etc., bake in the hot oven for 5-7 minutes, or until brown, then leave to cool.

Put all the ingredients for lemon curd into an enamel pan or stone jam jar standing in boiling water. Stir gently over low heat until mixture is thick. (It must not boil or it will curdle.) Pour into a bowl and allow to cool.

When all the pastry is cool, brush with warm apricot glaze and mount one ring on top of another on a base. Each gâteau has one plain circle as a base and two rings. Brush the top and sides of each gâteau with apricot glaze and decorate with the small pastry shapes, crystallised fruit or chopped nuts.

To serve: reserve a little cream for decoration and whip the remainder until it begins to thicken, then fold in the lemon curd. Divide between the gateaux and decorate the top with rosettes of whipped cream, crystallised fruit and chopped nuts.

21st birthday fruit cake

1¼ lb plain flour
1 teaspoon salt
2 teaspoons cinnamon
2 teaspoons mixed spice
pinch of grated nutmeg
1 lb seedless raisins
1 lb seeded raisins (chopped)
2 lb sultanas
1½ lb currants
½ lb candied peel (finely
   chopped, or shredded)
½ lb glacé cherries (halved)
½ lb almonds (blanched and
   shredded)
1 lb butter
1 lb soft brown sugar
2 tablespoons black treacle
12 eggs
4 oz plain chocolate
¼ pint brandy, or sherry, or
   cider, or fruit juice
1 rounded teaspoon bicarbonate
   of soda
1 dessertspoon warm water

12-inch square cake tin

Method

Prepare the cake tin by lining it with 2-3 thicknesses of grease-proof paper and tying a stout band of brown paper or several thicknesses of newspaper around the outside of the tin. Do not grease the inside paper at all as the cake mixture is very rich and will not stick. Set the oven at 300°F or Mark 3.

Sift the flour, salt and spices together, divide into three portions; mix one portion with the prepared fruit and nuts. Soften the butter with a wooden spoon, add the sugar, beat until light and fluffy, then stir in the black treacle. Separate the eggs, cream yolks until thick and add to butter mixture, alternately, with the second portion of flour.

Melt the chocolate on a plate over a pan of hot water and fold it into the mixture with the first portion of flour (mixed with the fruit and nuts) and brandy, or sherry, or cider, or fruit juice. Whisk the egg whites until stiff and fold them into the mixture with the remaining portion of flour. Dissolve the bicarbonate of soda in the warm water and stir this gently into the mixture.

Turn cake mixture into the prepared tin, smooth the top with a palette knife and brush with a very little water. This helps to keep the cake soft on the top in spite of the long baking. Put the cake in oven and bake for about 4-4½ hours. When the cake is nicely coloured (after about 1½ hours), cover with a double thickness of greaseproof paper and reduce oven to 290°F or Mark 2. Test the cake after 4 hours' cooking with a fine skewer; if it comes out quite clean, the cake is done.

Leave the cake to cool for about 30 minutes in the tin, then carefully turn it on to a wire cooling rack. When cold, wrap in several sheets of grease-proof paper and store in an airtight tin for at least 1 month before using. Cover with almond paste 2 weeks before using, then ice 1 week later.

21st birthday fruit cake continued

Adding chocolate to cake mixture with first portion of flour

Folding stiff egg whites into the cake with remaining flour

Rich almond paste

2½ lb ground almonds
1 lb icing sugar
1½ lb caster sugar
2 eggs
2 egg yolks
juice of ½ lemon
2 tablespoons brandy, or rum, or sherry
½ teaspoon vanilla essence
2 drops of almond essence
2 teaspoons orange flower water

Cover the cake with almond paste a week before icing to give it time to set. You will need 5 lb of paste.
For instructions on how to place it on the cake, see Christmas Fare page 14.

Royal icing

2 lb icing sugar
4 egg whites
2 teaspoons lemon juice, or orange flower water
½ teaspoon glycerine

Allow 2 lb icing sugar for covering and piping on the cake and then use boiled marzipan for the decoration.

Method

Pass the icing sugar through a fine nylon or hair sieve; whisk the egg whites to a froth and add the icing sugar, a spoonful at a time, beating thoroughly between each addition. Stir in the flavouring and glycerine and continue beating until the icing will stand in peaks. When using the icing for coating, piping and decorating cakes, keep the bowl covered with a damp cloth to prevent a crust forming on the top.

Boiled marzipan

1 lb granulated sugar
6 fl oz and 1 teaspoon water
¾ lb ground almonds
2 egg whites (lightly beaten)
juice of ½ lemon
1 teaspoon orange flower water
3-4 tablespoons icing sugar
pink colouring

*Sugar thermometer; 1-inch diameter
plain cutter; forcing bag. No 2
plain writing pipe and a shell pipe*

This almond paste is almost white and colours well for cake decorating.

Method

Place the sugar and water in a saucepan and dissolve over gentle heat; bring it to the boil and cook steadily to 240°F. Remove the pan from the heat and beat the syrup until it looks a little cloudy, stir in the ground almonds, add the egg whites and cook over a gentle heat for 2-3 minutes. Add the flavourings and turn on to a marble slab or laminated surface dusted with icing sugar.

When the marzipan is cool, knead it until quite smooth. Divide it in half, colour one piece pale pink, the other piece a deeper pink. Roll both out thinly and cut into rounds with the cutter. Make a number of cone-shaped bases and curl the prepared petals round them (see illustration, right).
Build up with 2-3 petals for buds, or 5-6 petals for full-blown roses, mixing the shades of pink, if liked.

To decorate fruit cake

Arrange marzipan flowers on cake. Finish the top and bottom edges with a piped double trellis of royal icing; place roses in the bottom corners. Put the ribbon across the cake diagonally with the key on top, and arrange some artificial fern naturally among the flowers.

Curling a petal round a base made from boiled marzipan. Use 2-3 petals to make a bud

Building up the petals to form decorative flower heads. Use 5-6 petals for full-blown rose

129

Fresh fruit salad

2 oranges
2 clementines
3 ripe pears
8 oz grapes
3 bananas

For sugar syrup
3 oz sugar
1 strip lemon rind, or piece of
  vanilla pod
6 tablespoons water
2-3 tablespoons liqueur
  (kirsch, or maraschino) — optional

Method

First prepare sugar syrup; dissolve sugar slowly in the water, add lemon rind or vanilla pod and boil for 1 minute. Tip into a bowl and leave to cool.

Cut peel, pith and first skin from oranges with a sharp, serrated-edge knife to expose flesh; then remove segments by cutting between each membrane. Peel and slice clementines. Peel and quarter pears, remove core, cut each quarter into two. Pip grapes by hooking out pips with eye of a trussing needle. Only white grapes should be peeled, not black ones. If skin is difficult to remove from white grapes, dip them into boiling water for 1 minute. Peel bananas and cut in thick, slanting slices.

Moisten fruit with sugar syrup, add liqueur and turn fruit over carefully. Set a plate on top to keep fruit covered by the syrup. Chill before serving.

Hallowe'en

Our choice of dishes for Hallowe'en is designed to go with traditional games such as ducking for apples etc... The recipes, all of which serve 8, are arranged so that most of the food can be eaten with your fingers if wished. Some recipes for savoury tarts are given as well as other dishes suitable for a party of this kind.

Les crudités (Raw vegetable salad)

carrots
beetroot
swedes (preferably Cornish)
cabbage (drumhead, or Dutch)
celery
about ½ pint French dressing (see
    page 40)
1 bunch of watercress

This salad can be served with
Scotch eggs or dry devilled
chicken, and should be prepared 1 hour before serving.

Method
Grate the carrot, beetroot and
swedes separately on a fine
grater and put each vegetable
into separate bowls. Finely
shred the cabbage and celery
separately and put into separate
bowls. Moisten each vegetable
with French dressing and carefully arrange each kind in
sections in a large wooden or
china salad bowl.

    Set a bunch of watercress in
the centre and serve the salad
with hot rolls or a hot garlic loaf.
Hand a bowl of boiled dressing
separately.

*Some of the Hallowe'en dishes
to be found on the following pages :*

onion tart, *les crudités*, tomato tart, *and mulled red wine.*

Have rolls to fill up hungry corners, and apples for ducking

Tomato tart

For rich shortcrust pastry (see page 28)
8 oz plain flour
pinch of salt
4 oz butter
2 oz lard
1 egg yolk
2-3 tablespoons water

For filling
$4\frac{1}{2}$ oz fresh breadcrumbs
8 tomatoes
6 oz grated cheese (Cheddar, or Gruyère)
$\frac{1}{4}$ pint double cream
1 tablespoon chopped mixed herbs and parsley
1 dessertspoon anchovy essence
salt and pepper
grate of nutmeg (optional)

8-9 inch diameter flan ring

To make Fresh Breadcrumbs. Slice the bread and leave it exposed to the air for three or four days, then run through a wire sieve.

Method

Make up the pastry and chill well. Line it into the flan ring, making sure that there is a good edge standing up $\frac{1}{4}$ inch- above the ring. Prick the bottom with a fork and set aside to chill. Set the oven at 400°F or Mark 6.

Meanwhile prepare the filling: lightly brown the crumbs in the oven. Scald and skin the tomatoes, cut them in half, remove the stalk and seeds. Sprinkle tomatoes well with salt and leave them to stand for about 30 minutes. Tip off any liquid and dry the halves well.

Scatter the browned crumbs into the bottom of the flan, arrange the tomatoes on top in a single layer, rounded sides uppermost, mix the cheese and cream together with the herbs and anchovy essence. Season well and add a little grating of nutmeg. Spoon this mixture over the tomatoes and bake tart in the pre-set hot oven for 30-40 minutes.

If the tart is browning too quickly after 25 minutes, lower the oven to 350°F or Mark 4 and continue to cook until the pastry shrinks slightly from the flan ring. Then remove the ring, and put the tart back into the oven for a few minutes. Serve hot or cold.

Leek and bacon pie

12 oz quantity of puff pastry
   (home-made, see page 10, or bought)

For filling
10 leeks
10 oz green streaky bacon
$\frac{1}{2}$ pint chicken, or veal, stock
3 eggs
salt and pepper
4-5 tablespoons single cream,
   or creamy milk
1 egg (beaten)

8$\frac{1}{2}$-9 inch diameter pie plate

Method

First prepare the filling: trim the leeks, wash them well and cut into $\frac{3}{4}$-1 inch diagonal slices. Put these into a pan of boiling salted water, boil gently for 4-5 minutes, then drain them very well.

Remove any rind and rust from the bacon and cut into lardons. Put them in a pan with the water, bring to the boil, drain, rinse and drain them again.

Break the eggs into a bowl, beat with a fork, season and add the cream (or milk). Add the leeks and bacon, moisten with stock and set aside. Set the oven at 400°F or Mark 6.

Take about half of the pastry, roll it out very thinly and line into the pie plate, making sure that it overlaps the edge slightly. Prick the bottom with a fork and turn the leek mixture into this. Roll out the other half of the pastry to about $\frac{1}{4}$ inch thick, press down around the edges and trim. Mark the top of the pastry with the back of the knife, roll out the trimmings and make either leaves, rose or tassel for decoration.

Scallop the edge of the pie with your fingers, brush over with the beaten egg, chill for 5-10 minutes, then bake in pre-set hot oven for about 25 minutes or until pastry is a good russet-brown and well risen. Serve hot.

Watchpoint Before baking put a baking sheet into the oven for a few minutes to get thoroughly hot. Then set the pie plate on this so that the bottom of the tart will be well cooked from the additional heat from the baking sheet.

Lardons are strips of bacon fat or belly pork, cut about $\frac{1}{4}$ inch thick and $1\frac{1}{4}$ inches long.

Onion tart

For rich shortcrust pastry

8 oz plain flour
pinch of salt and pepper
4 oz butter
2 oz lard
1 egg yolk
2-3 tablespoons cold water

For filling

4 large onions (finely sliced)
3 oz butter
6-8 rashers of streaky bacon
  (diced)
3 large eggs
$\frac{1}{4}$ pint creamy milk
$2\frac{1}{2}$ fl oz cream, or evaporated
  milk
2-3 tablespoons Parmesan
  cheese
a little melted butter

9-inch diameter flan ring

Method

Prepare the pastry (see page 28). Chill it, then roll out and line into the flan ring, making sure that the edge stands up $\frac{1}{4}$ inch above the ring. Prick the bottom with a fork and chill.

Meanwhile prepare the filling; slice the onions finely, blanch, drain well and then return to the pan with the butter. Cook them until golden and quite tender, then tip into a bowl. Blanch the diced bacon and fry until crisp in the butter left in the pan from the onions. Add all to onions.

Beat the eggs with a fork, season, add milk and cream (or evaporated milk), then add to the onion mixture. Pour filling into the tart, sprinkle with Parmesan cheese and a little melted butter and bake in a hot oven, pre-set at 400°F or Mark 6, for 10-12 minutes to set the pastry; then lower the heat to 375°F or Mark 5 and continue to cook for a further 20 minutes or until the egg mixture is golden-brown and set. (Pre-heat and bake onion tart on baking sheet as for leek and bacon, pie-see page 135).

Dry devilled chicken

chicken drumsticks, or legs
   (allow 2 per person)
2 onions (sliced)
2 carrots (sliced)
bouquet garni
½ teaspoon black peppercorns
salt

For devil mixture
4 oz butter
2 tablespoons tomato ketchup
2 tablespoons Worcestershire
   sauce
1 teaspoon ground mace
2 tablespoons chutney (either
   home-made tomato, or ready-
   made mango)
salt
black pepper
dash of anchovy essence
cayenne pepper, or Tabasco
   sauce (optional)
cutlet frills and watercress to
   garnish (optional)

Method

Put the drumsticks into a large pan with the sliced vegetables, bouquet garni, peppercorns and water barely to cover. Salt lightly, cover pan and cook gently for about 15 minutes. Cool chicken slightly in the liquid.

Meanwhile prepare the devil mixture : cream butter thoroughly and gradually mix in remaining ingredients. If the devil mixture is to be a hot one, season with cayenne pepper (or a dash of Tabasco sauce).

Take up chicken pieces, drain well and strip off the skin. Then spread a little of the devil mixture on each piece.

Pre-heat the grill and cook chicken in grill pan until well browned (about 6 minutes), turning the pieces once.

Watchpoint During grilling, spread pieces with the rest of the devil mixture and baste with any drippings from pan.

Allow the pieces to cool slightly, then place a cutlet frill on the end of each bone. Serve devilled chicken with watercress or hand a bowl of watercress separately.

Scotch eggs

8 new laid eggs (hard-boiled)
1 lb pork sausage meat
1 tablespoon chopped mixed
   herbs
salt and pepper
seasoned flour
1 egg (beaten)
dried white breadcrumbs (for
   frying)
deep fat (for frying)

Method

Mix the sausage meat with the herbs and seasoning. Have the eggs ready peeled and dried. Divide the sausage meat into equal portions. Pat these out into rounds on a dampened board, place an egg on each one and fold the sausage meat up around the egg to envelop it completely. Roll eggs in seasoned flour, brush with beaten egg and coat well with the crumbs.

Fry the Scotch eggs in deep fat until a russet-brown. Cool them before cutting in half to serve.

Top : moulding seasoned sausage meat round hard-boiled eggs. Above : lifting Scotch eggs into deep fat after coating

Veal, ham and egg pie

For raised pie pastry
2 lb plain flour
2 egg yolks (optional)
12 fl oz warm water, or milk
12 oz good lard
salt and pepper

For filling
2 lb boiled piece of collar of
  bacon (either green or smoked,
  according to taste)
1¾ lb minced pie veal
good pinch of ground mace
1 dessertspoon grated onion
5 hard-boiled eggs

*Raised pie mould, about 12-14
  inches long*

This recipe serves 8-10 people.

Method

Skin the bacon, cutting away any rust, then put all through a mincer and weigh. There should be approximately 1¾ lb. Mix this with the minced veal, ground mace and chopped onion. Set this filling aside and set oven at 400°F or Mark 6.

To prepare raised pie pastry: sift flour and seasoning into a bowl and make a well in the centre. Mix egg yolks with a little of the warm liquid. Add the lard to the rest of the liquid and bring it to the boil; pour this into the centre of the flour and work well with a wooden spoon. When heat of liquid has lessened, pour in egg mixture. **Watchpoint** This pastry does not keep well when raw and should never be chilled. Use immediately after making.

As soon as mixture becomes a paste, turn it out on to your floured work surface and knead it very lightly. Roll it out, re-serving one-quarter of pastry for the top, and line into pie mould, or mould it around a 2 lb jam jar. Fill mould with half of the filling, lay peeled hard-boiled eggs down the centre, and cover with rest of filling. Roll out reserved pastry, together with any trimmings, and cover top of pie.

To decorate, brush top with beaten egg, then bake pie in hot oven, pre-set at 400°F or Mark 6, for about 40 minutes. Then wrap a double sheet of greaseproof paper over the top of and around the pie. Lower heat to 350°F or Mark 4 and continue cooking for 50 minutes. Then take out pie and leave to cool. Take off mould while pie is still warm. When cold, cut in slices to serve.

Russian pancakes

$\frac{3}{4}$ pint pancake batter (see box below)

For filling
1 small chicken (about $2\frac{1}{2}$ lb)
root vegetables (for poaching)
bouquet garni
6 oz cooked ham (sliced and shredded)

For béchamel sauce
2 oz butter
2 oz flour
$\frac{3}{4}$ pint flavoured milk
salt and pepper

For coating
beaten egg
dried white crumbs
oil, or lard, or dripping (for frying)

Pancake batter

To make a $\frac{3}{4}$ pint quantity of batter, use 6 oz plain flour, pinch of salt, 2 eggs and 2 dessertspoons melted butter or salad oil to $\frac{3}{4}$ pint milk. Sift the flour with the salt into a bowl, make a well in the centre, add the eggs and begin to add the milk slowly, stirring all the time. When half the milk has been added, stir in the melted butter or oil and beat well until smooth.

Add the remaining milk and leave to stand for 30 minutes before using. The batter should have the consistency of thin cream — if too thick, add a little extra milk.

Method

First prepare the filling. Poach the chicken, with root vegetables to flavour and the bouquet garni, in enough water barely to cover. Allow it to cool in the liquid. Then skin, take the meat from the carcass, cut into shreds and add the ham.

Prepare the béchamel sauce (see page 9). Work sauce into the meat and allow to get cold.

Meanwhile prepare about 18-20 thin pancakes. When these are made, spread them out on a board. Put 1 tablespoon of the filling into each one and fold up like a parcel. Seal the edges with a little beaten egg, then brush with beaten egg and roll in the crumbs, pressing them on well.

Fry the pancakes until golden-brown in the deep fat, which should come half way up the pancakes. When golden-brown, turn them carefully with a palette knife and allow to brown on the other side. Then take them out and place on a cooling rack set over a baking sheet. When ready to serve slide these into a hot oven (pre-set at 450°F or Mark 7) and heat through. Serve pancakes hot.

Chocolate nut cake

6 egg whites
pinch of salt
13 oz caster sugar
7 oz browned hazelnuts
1½ teaspoons vinegar
2-3 drops of vanilla essence

For filling
½ pint double cream

For chocolate sauce
8 oz plain chocolate
12 fl oz water
5 oz granulated sugar

To decorate
icing sugar
extra whipped cream (optional)

Two 9-inch diameter sandwich tins

Method

Grease and flour tins and line bottoms with greaseproof paper. Set oven at 350°F or Mark 4.

First prepare the cake. Whip the whites with a pinch of salt to a really firm snow. Then gradually add the caster sugar; continuing to whisk the mixture until it stands in peaks.

Brown hazelnuts by baking for 5-6 minutes in a hot oven, then rub the nuts thoroughly in a rough cloth to remove the skins and grind the kernels through a nut mill.

Fold nuts into mixture with vinegar and vanilla, then turn into prepared sandwich tins. Bake in pre-set moderate oven for 35 minutes, then take out and leave for a few minutes before turning out.

Break up or grate chocolate for sauce and put into a pan with the water. Stir it over gentle heat until dissolved, then add the sugar and boil gently, with the pan uncovered, for about 15 minutes or until it has the consistency of cream. Pour off chocolate into a bowl, dust with caster sugar, cover with dampened greaseproof paper, to prevent a skin from forming, and leave to get cold.

Lightly whip the cream and fold in 2-3 tablespoons of chocolate sauce to flavour it well. Spread this on one half of the cake, place the other half on top and press together lightly.

Leave cake overnight in the refrigerator, or chill for several hours. Then dust top with icing sugar and decorate with extra whipped cream. Serve with chocolate sauce.

Apple bonfire

8-10 even-size apples
(preferably Cox's)
grated rind and juice of 1 lemon
4-5 tablespoons mincemeat
1-2 tablespoons sherry, or cider
$\frac{1}{4}$ pint water
3 tablespoons granulated sugar
5-7 sugar lumps
2-3 tablespoons brandy, or
sherry

Method

Remove the cores from the apples, then set them in a deep ovenproof casserole with lid. Mix the grated rind and juice of a lemon with the mincemeat, moisten with a little sherry (or cider) and fill this into the centres of the apples. Boil the water and sugar together to make a light syrup, then pour round the apples.

Cover apples with a buttered paper and the lid and cook in oven, pre-set at 350°F or Mark 4, for about 20-25 minutes, or until tender, basting well. Cool apples a little, then pile them up in a shallow ovenproof dish. Soak the sugar lumps with brandy (or sherry) and place them here and there on the apples. Reduce any syrup left in the dish and pour round.

To serve: set fire to the brandy-soaked sugar lumps and serve at once.

Watchpoint It is most important that the sugar should be thoroughly impregnated with the spirit, and brandy will give a much better, longer lasting flame than sherry.

Mulled red wine

For each bottle of red wine allow:
4-6 oz sugar lumps
pared rind of 1 lemon
2-inch stick of cinnamon
2 cloves
blade of mace
slices of lemon (for serving)

Method

Put the wine and sugar into a large pan. Set on a gentle heat until the sugar has dissolved, then add the lemon rind and spices. Bring it slowly to simmering point or until the surface is covered with white foam, then draw pan aside.

Have ready some warmed glasses and a jug. Strain the wine into the jug then pour into the glasses.

Watchpoint Be careful not to have the mulled wine too hot or else the glasses may crack.

Put a slice of lemon into each glass and serve.

Lambs' wool

3 quarts of brown ale
1$\frac{1}{2}$ pints sweet white wine
$\frac{1}{2}$ grated nutmeg
1 teaspoon ground ginger
1 stick of cinnamon
4-5 baked apples
brown sugar (to taste)

Method

Heat the ale, wine and spices together in a large pan. Skin the apples and mash them to a pulp with a fork; pour over the liquid, first removing the cinnamon. Mix together well, then run mixture through a strainer, pressing it well. Add sugar to taste and reheat. Drink hot.

Guy Fawkes

Special bonfire night food certainly helps the festivities along and here we give recipes for party food for children, and for teenagers.

For young children

For small children, we suggest a light tea of 'flower' sandwiches and butterscotch cracknels. They could then be sent into the garden for the firework display, each provided with a greaseproof bag full of hot chips and chipolata sausages. Allow about 3 chipolatas for each child and 2-3 times that quantity of chips (which could be bought from the local shop).

After the festivities, they can return to the house to hot blackcurrant punch, gingerbread men, or a gingerbread house, and — a firm favourite with children — cubes of cheese and pineapple secured with cocktail sticks.

Flower sandwiches

These may be made from a milk loaf or close-textured brown bread. Slice the bread and stamp rounds with a cutter 2-2$\frac{1}{2}$ inches in diameter. Butter the rounds, or spread them with curd cheese. Arrange on each a 'flower' picture. For example, a marguerite can be made with the chopped white and yolk of a hard-boiled egg, with cucumber skin for stems and leaves. A flowerpot can be made with tomato or pimiento, with watercress leaves and chopped prawns, or whole shrimps, forming a plant.

Butterscotch craknels

5$\frac{1}{2}$ oz soft brown sugar
1 tablespoon golden syrup
$\frac{3}{4}$ oz butter
$\frac{1}{2}$ cup milk
3 oz cornflakes

This quantity makes about 18 cracknels.

Method
Cook the sugar, syrup, butter and milk together, in a pan over gentle heat, until the mixture forms a ball when a teaspoonful is dropped into a cup of cold water.

Lightly toast the cornflakes, put them in a buttered bowl, add the sugar mixture and mix thoroughly. Put out as quickly as possible, a teaspoonful at a time, on a buttered baking sheet. Leave until quite cold before taking cracknels off the tin.

Hot blackcurrant punch

Use Ribena and dilute to taste with boiling water, add one slice of orange and half a slice of lemon to each glass.

Gingerbread foundation

- 1 lb plain flour
- 1 tablespoon bicarbonate of soda
- $\frac{1}{2}$ teaspoon salt
- 1 dessertspoon ground ginger
- $\frac{1}{2}$ teaspoon ground cinnamon
- 4 oz butter
- 8 oz soft brown sugar
- 1 teacup black treacle
- about 2 tablespoons evaporated milk

Method

Sift the flour with the soda, salt and spices into a mixing bowl. Place the butter, sugar and treacle in a saucepan and stir over gentle heat until dissolved. Allow this to cool a little, then mix it into the flour with enough evaporated milk to give a firm dough. Chill the mixture for 30 minutes before rolling out and shaping as required.

Gingerbread house

gingerbread foundation (as recipe left)
little sugar syrup (see page 10)
royal icing

Forcing bag and writing nozzle

Method

Set oven at 325°F or Mark 3. Grease several baking sheets.

Cut out a paper guide as follows: for long walls, 1 rectangle 5 inches by 10 inches; for roof, 1 rectangle 4 inches by 10 inches; for side walls, 1 piece, basically 5 inches square rising to a gable with 4-inch sides (see page 146); for chimney, a 2-inch square.

Roll out gingerbread to about $\frac{1}{8}$ inch thick. Use paper guide to cut out 4 walls, 2 roof pieces and 4 chimney pieces. Place sections carefully on baking sheets and bake in pre-set oven for 10-15 minutes.

When cold, using the forcing bag and writing tube, decorate with royal icing, marking the windows and doors, and the tiles on the roof. Join the pieces together by dipping the edges in sugar syrup boiled to 280°F or the 'small crack' stage.
Note : cut V-shaped pieces out of base of side-pieces of chimney so that it fits on roof.

Then cover the joins with icing, using forcing bag without the writing pipe.

Gingerbread men

gingerbread foundation (as recipe
   page 145)

For decoration
currants
glacé cherries
white royal icing

Forcing bag and writing tube

The 1 lb quantity of foundation
makes 3-4 dozen gingerbread
men, about $3\frac{1}{2}$ inches high.

Method
Set oven at 325°F or Mark 3.
Grease several baking sheets.
   Roll out the mixture a good
$\frac{1}{4}$ inch thick. Cut out a card-
board gingerbread man pattern;
grease the underside, lay it on
the dough and cut round it with
a small sharp knife. When all the
gingerbread men are cut, lift
them up carefully with a palette
knife and place them on the
prepared baking sheets. Press
currants in to make the eyes and
waistcoat buttons and a small
piece of glacé cherry for the
mouth.
   Bake in pre-set oven for
10-15 minutes; cool slightly
and then carefully remove them
from the baking sheet. With a
little white icing and a writing
tube, outline eyebrows, nose,
tie, belt, cuffs and shoes.

*Guy Fawkes party fare for small
children; gingerbread house and*

Guy Fawkes

gingerbread men ; cheese and flower sandwiches ; butterscotch pineapple on sticks ; platter of cracknels ; blackcurrant punch

For older children

As this party will no doubt be at suppertime rather than teatime, we suggest serving assiette anglaise with Catherine-wheel salad or, as an alternative, kebabs with jacket potatoes. After the party, serve tomato soup with baked beans added to it (1 large can of beans to 2 quarts of soup), so that it is fairly thick and very sustaining.

Mulligatawny soup

3 pints mutton, or chicken, stock
1 large cooking apple
$1\frac{1}{2}$ oz butter
2 carrots (sliced)
2 onions (sliced)
2 sticks of celery (sliced)
1 oz flour
1 tablespoon curry powder
salt and pepper
juice of $\frac{1}{2}$ lemon
1 dessertspoon arrowroot, or cornflour (optional)

Method
Peel, core and chop the apple. Melt the butter, add sliced vegetables and cook slowly until soft but not coloured, then stir in the flour and curry powder and brown slowly. Tip on the stock, season, add the apple and stir until boiling, then simmer for 1 hour. Strain the soup, return it to the pan and add the lemon juice. Taste for seasoning. If necessary, add a little extra thickening (slaked arrowroot or cornflour); reboil, simmer to a syrupy consistency.

Omelet loaf

Split a French loaf lengthways and remove the soft crumb. Spread well with 2 oz mustard-flavoured butter, then line with sliced ham. Fill the cavity with one large omelet (made with 4-6 eggs), cover this with more ham and put back the top of the loaf. Wrap it in foil to keep it fresh, and slice as needed.

Chicken-in-a-basket

Use a fairly shallow wicker basket, such as a large bread basket. Line it first with foil and then with crisp lettuce leaves.

Roast chickens in the usual way, allow them to cool and then cut into joints. Arrange joints in the basket; in the middle place a container holding a mayonnaise flavoured with mustard or tomato chutney.

Cover with foil and pack on the top plenty of paper napkins so that the chicken joints can be held with the fingers and dunked in the mayonnaise.

Assiette anglaise

This is a platter of assorted cold meats. A good selection would be : ham; brisket of beef, or cold roast beef; salami, or liver sausage; and corned beef, or tongue.

Catherine-wheel salad

Foundation dough

8 oz flour
$\frac{1}{2}$ teaspoon salt
$\frac{1}{2}$ oz yeast
1 teaspoon sugar
$2\frac{1}{2}$ fl oz milk (warmed)
2 eggs (beaten)
2 oz butter (creamed)
extra butter and little French
   mustard, or cream cheese
   (flavoured to taste)

For topping

beetroot (coarsely grated)
French dressing
cucumber (thinly sliced)
carrot (grated)
tomatoes (skinned, thinly sliced)
onion (cut into rings and
   blanched)
coleslaw

Method

Sift the flour and salt in a warmed mixing bowl. Cream the yeast and sugar and add this to the warmed milk with the beaten eggs. Then add all the liquid to the flour and beat thoroughly. Work the creamed butter into the paste. Cover and leave for 40 minutes to rise.

Set the oven at 400°F or Mark 6. Pat out the dough on to a floured baking sheet in as large a round as possible. Allow to prove for 15 minutes, then bake in pre-set oven for about 30 minutes.

When cold, split the round in two and sandwich with the extra butter, flavoured with French mustard, or with the flavoured creamed cheese.

Start arranging the salads in the centre and work out towards the edge, beginning with the beetroot, mixed with a little French dressing. Surround this with the cucumber, then grated carrot. Then arrange the tomato slices, overlapping them, and between each slice place a thinly cut onion ring. Round the tomatoes, arrange the coleslaw. Continue in this way until the whole surface is covered.

Brochettes of kidney

Allow one skewer per person and for each skewer the following ingredients :

2 lambs kidneys
2 or 3 squares of lambs liver
boiled rice (for serving)
chopped parsley (to garnish)

For marinade
$2\frac{1}{2}$ fl oz olive oil
2-3 tablespoons red wine
few sprigs of thyme
salt
pepper (ground from mill)

Cutting liver into squares and marinating the skinned and split kidneys for the brochettes·

Method

Skin and split kidneys, cut the liver into 1-1$\frac{1}{2}$ inch squares and remove the ducts. Marinate the liver and kidneys in the mixture of oil and red wine, adding seasoning and the thyme. Leave for 2-3 hours.

Thread the kidneys and liver alternately on to skewers and grill for 6-8 minutes, moistening with the marinade throughout the cooking time.

Serve brochettes on a bed of boiled rice and sprinkle with chopped parsley. Serve with bowl of crisp bacon rolls.

Threading the liver and kidney on to skewers (see photograph of the finished dish opposite)

Marinate To soak raw meat game / fish. in cooked or raw spiced liquid (marinade) of wine, oil, herbs and vegetables for hours / days before cooking. This softens, tenderises and flavours, and a marinade can be used for final sauce. Use glass / glazed / enamel / stainless steel vessel to withstand effects of acid.

Plum and walnut cake

1 lb seedless raisins
4 tablespoons brandy
6 oz plain flour
2 oz self-raising flour
pinch of salt
8 oz walnuts
4 oz glacé cherries (halved)
8 oz butter
8 oz soft brown sugar
4 eggs

Savarin mould (1½-2 pints capacity)

Method
Put the seedless raisins in an airtight container with the brandy and leave overnight.

Set oven at 350°F or Mark 4. Butter and flour the mould.

Sift the flours together with the salt. Reserve about half the nuts for the top of the cake, chop the rest and mix with soaked raisins, glacé cherries and one-third of the flour. Cream the butter until soft, add the sugar and beat until light and creamy. Then beat in the eggs and fold in half the remaining flour. Add the soaked raisins, fruit and flour mixture, and finally the rest of the flour. Turn mixture into the prepared mould and bake in pre-set oven for about 1½ hours.

Beef hot pot

4 lb skirt of beef
1 lb onions
½ lb mushrooms
1-2 tablespoons dripping
1-2 tablespoons flour
1 pint brown ale
¾ pint good stock
1 teaspoon sugar
1 teaspoon wine vinegar
salt
pepper (ground from mill)
2 lb potatoes
melted butter

Method
Set oven at 350°F or Mark 4.

Cut the meat into even-sized pieces, about 1½ inches square. Slice the onions, wash and trim the mushrooms and cut them in half. Heat the dripping in a large flameproof casserole and put in just enough meat to cover the base. When beef is nicely coloured, turn it; when brown all over, remove it and put in more meat to brown in the same way. Reduce the heat under the pan, add the onions and cook slowly until golden-brown. Dust in enough flour to absorb the fat left in the pan and leave this to colour lightly. Add the beer and stock and stir until boiling. Add the sugar and the wine vinegar, replace the meat and season. Cover pan tightly and cook in pre-set moderate oven for 2 hours.

Peel and slice the potatoes. Then add mushrooms to the hot pot and put potato slices on top of the meat, baste them with the juice in the pan and then brush the top with a little melted butter. Return the casserole, uncovered, to the oven and continue cooking for about another 45 minutes.

Teenage Parties

Teenage Party food should always be satisfying and easy to eat.
For the older groups we suggest some form of participation in
cooking the food as this will add to their enjoyment. All recipes
given are for 6 people and can of course be made for
larger numbers by increasing the quantities.

Prawn flan

For rich shortcrust pastry

8 oz flour
4 oz butter
2 oz shortening
1 egg yolk
2 tablespoons water (to mix)

For filling

8 oz shelled prawns
4 eggs (hard-boiled)
¼ pint mayonnaise
1 small cucumber
black pepper
1 tablespoon chopped dill, or chives
6 anchovy fillets
2-3 tablespoons milk

8-9 inch diameter flan ring

Method
Prepare the pastry (see page 28) and set aside to chill for about 30 minutes. Roll it out and line into the flan ring and bake blind for about 15 minutes.

Meanwhile prepare the filling. Shred the egg whites and mix with the prawns and mayonnaise. Sieve the egg yolks, cover and set aside. Cut the cucumber into small dice, sprinkle lightly with salt and cover; keep in a cool place for 30 minutes, then drain, season with black pepper and add the herbs. Divide the anchovy fillets in half lengthways and soak in the milk to remove the excess salt.

When the pastry case is cool, fill with the prawn mixture and arrange a thick border of cucumber around the edge. Fill the centre with sieved egg yolk and cover with a lattice of anchovy fillets. Serve cold.

Tarte au poisson

For rich shortcrust pastry

8 oz flour
4 oz butter
1 oz shortening
1 egg yolk
2-3 tablespoons water (to mix)

For filling

7 oz can tunny fish (flaked)
4 tomatoes
1 oz butter
2-3 onions (finely sliced)
½ oz flour
¼ pint milk
salt and pepper
grated nutmeg
2 eggs (beaten)
2 oz grated cheese

8-inch diameter flan ring

Less shortening is used than in the previous recipe in order to make the tart less rich.

Method
First prepare the rich shortcrust pastry (see page 28) and chill. Roll out pastry and line into a plain or fluted flan ring and bake blind for about 15 minutes. Meanwhile scald and skin tomatoes, cut in half, remove seeds, and set flesh on one side.

Melt the butter in a pan, add the onions and cook until soft. Mix in the flour and add the milk. Stir sauce until boiling, draw aside and add seasoning, nutmeg, and beaten eggs. Arrange the tomatoes and flaked tunny fish in the bottom of the flan, season, and pour in the sauce to fill well.

Scatter with grated cheese and put into the oven, pre-set at 350°F or Mark 4, until well set and golden-brown (about 30 minutes). Serve warm.

Hamburger bun

2 lb plain flour
1 teaspoon salt
1 pint skimmed milk
1 oz yeast
4 oz butter
2 tablespoons caster sugar
little milk (to finish)

This quantity makes 30-40 buns.

Method

Sift the flour with the salt into a mixing bowl. Warm the milk to blood heat, add the yeast, butter and sugar, and stir until dissolved. Pour mixture at once into the centre of the flour and mix to a smooth dough. Put the dough into a greased bowl, cover with a damp cloth and set to rise in a warm place for 1 hour, or until double in bulk.

Turn the dough on to a floured board, divide into equal portions and knead into small balls. Flatten these with the palm of your hand, set them on a greased and floured baking sheet and prove for 10 minutes. Brush the tops with milk and cook for 15-20 minutes in a pre-set oven, 429°F or Mark 7.

While still hot rub the top of each bun with buttery paper.

Hamburgers

1½ lb finely ground hamburger mince, or 1½ lb blade bone, steak, or a cut from the aitch-bone (mince it yourself)
6 tablespoons fresh breadcrumbs
¼ teaspoon dried thyme
½ teaspoon salt
pepper (ground from mill)
1 egg (beaten)

Method

Mix the breadcrumbs, thyme and seasoning with the mince, then add the beaten egg slowly and work together very well. Shape into flat cakes about ½ inch thick and the same diameter as the buns (they will then need only 3-4 minutes frying or grilling on each side).

For serving from the kitchen the buns should be split and hot hamburgers put in the centre. At the table the bun's 'hat' is removed and the accompaniments added as desired.

Fruit crust pies with apple or peach filling

For American pastry

7 oz lard, or shortening
4 tablespoons water
11 oz plain flour
$\frac{1}{4}$ teaspoon salt

For apple filling

2 lb Pippin apples (peeled and cored)
$\frac{1}{2}$ teaspoon freshly ground cinnamon
grated rind and juice of 1 lemon
little butter

For peach filling

1 large can sliced peaches
4 fresh peaches
little butter

Two 7-8 inch diameter pie plates

This quantity of pastry will make 2 pies.

Method

To make the American pastry, put the lard (or shortening) and water into a mixing bowl and work together with a wooden spoon until creamy. Sift the flour with the salt into the bowl and cut and stir with a round-bladed knife until all the ingredients are well blended. Gather the dough together with the fingertips, press it firmly into a ball, wrap it in waxed paper and chill before using.

Divide the pastry in four, and roll out two pieces into rounds about $\frac{1}{8}$ inch thick and 1 inch larger than the pie plates to allow for depth. Keep the pastry round as it is being rolled and be careful not to add extra flour as this will make it too tough. Fold the rounds in half, or lift them one at a time on the rolling pin, and quickly line them into the pie plates. Avoid stretching the pastry, and trim the edges with a knife or scissors.

Set the oven at 425°F or Mark 7. Slice the apples, and fill one of the pies, doming the fruit, and add the cinnamon and lemon juice.

For the other pie, drain the canned peaches well; scald, peel and slice the fresh peaches and mix them with the canned ones. Fill into the pie.

Dot both fruits with butter, and moisten the edges of the pastry with water.

Roll out the remaining pieces of pastry a little thinner than the bottom crusts and 1 inch larger than the plates. Fold in half. Make several slits near the centres, and lift them carefully on the pies. Unfold the pastry and fold the overhanging pastry under the lower layer. Seal the edges and flute with your forefinger and thumb.

Bake in the pre-set hot oven for 15 minutes, then reduce the heat to 400°F or Mark 6, and bake for a further 20-30 minutes. Serve warm.

Fruit crust pie, with peach filling, ▶
*is served à la mode with vanilla
ice cream*

Ice-cream variations

We suggest ice-cream, bought in several different flavours, as a sweet for teenage parties. Here are a few suggestions for serving it in a variety of ways.

Coffee ice-cream Serve this with broken walnuts, and maple syrup (which can be bought in bottles).
Chocolate ice-cream Serve with a sprinkling of crushed peppermint rock.
Banana split Arrange a scoop of vanilla and strawberry ice-cream in a banana, split in two. Add a little chocolate sauce and top with whipped cream and chopped nuts, like those served in a soda fountain.
Orange water ice Surround this with fresh strawberries and top with whipped cream.

Pineapple and chicken croquettes

1 lb cooked chicken (chopped finely and marinated in 3-4 tablespoons juice from the canned pineapple, and a squeeze of lemon)
4 oz fresh breadcrumbs
1 tablespoon chopped chives
salt and pepper
2 eggs (beaten)
6 pineapple rings (canned)
$\frac{1}{2}$ oz butter
2 tablespoons brown sugar
2 tablespoons pineapple juice (from canned rings)
squeeze of lemon
1 tablespoon chopped parsley (to garnish)

This quantity makes 6 large croquettes.

Method

Mix the marinated chicken meat, breadcrumbs and chives together; season, and bind with beaten egg.

Shape mixture into 6 rounds like cakes and place each on a pineapple ring, then set on a buttered baking dish.

Melt the $\frac{1}{2}$ oz butter in a small pan, add the brown sugar and blend in pineapple and lemon juice. Spoon this mixture over the croquettes and bake for 30-40 minutes in the oven, set at 375°F or Mark 5, basting from time to time. Serve garnished with chopped parsley.

For a special occasion you could arrange the croquettes on one side of a hot oval meat dish, and place on the other half of the dish beef and potato galettes. Serve both with a large bowl of pickled red cabbage and another of coleslaw salad.

Meat balls

1 lb minced raw beef
6 oz minced raw pork
1 cup (3 oz) fine dry breadcrumbs
2 oz grated Parmesan cheese
1 tablespoon chopped parsley
2 cloves of garlic (crushed with salt)
salt and pepper
2 eggs (beaten)
scant $\frac{1}{4}$ pint milk
seasoned flour
3 tablespoons dripping, or oil

For tomato and pepper sauce
2 large onions (chopped)
1 oz flour
1 can (14 oz) tomatoes
2 green peppers (core and seeds removed, flesh chopped)
salt, pepper and sugar (to taste)
dash of Worcestershire sauce
1 bayleaf

Method

Mix the meat, breadcrumbs, cheese, parsley, garlic, and seasonings, and bind with the beaten eggs and milk. Shape mixture into $1\frac{1}{2}$-inch balls and roll them in seasoned flour.

Melt about 3 tablespoons good dripping (or oil) in a pan and fry the meat balls a few at a time until golden-brown on all sides. Remove balls and keep warm. Add the onions to the pan and cook slowly until golden. Blend in the flour, followed by the remaining ingredients, and stir until boiling. Replace the meat balls, cover and simmer for 1 hour. Serve with plainly boiled spaghetti, tossed in butter and seasoned, allowing 2 oz pasta per person.